BOD

Phil Moulton is a former World Karate Champion and World Record holder. He is a Karate 8th Dan Black Belt with over twenty-five years' experience in bodyguarding and is one of the UK's most respected personal security and close protection specialists.

To All at the

Airport

# THE
# BODYGUARD

## PHIL MOULTON

My dream was to teach others how to look after themselves, and also to protect people who were being bullied or intimidated. I have had the privilege of protecting people from all over the world, and there is nothing more rewarding than knowing a person is safe because of the things you've put into place.

Phil Moulton
October 2018

Published by Phil Moulton
Urmston, Manchester

www.philmoultonassociates.co.uk

ISBN: 9781726686990

To all those with a dream, never give up.

# CONTENTS

# ACKNOWLEDGEMENTS

I would like to thank my wife, and best friend, Nadia, who has been there for me through thick and thin, who supported me and gave me the confidence to build a fantastic company. You are my love and my life.

Also, Callam and Thomas, my sons, both so different but I love you both equally as much. For my sister Elaine, who took over the role of my mum when she passed away. To my mum and late sister Diane, who aren't here, but of who my memories will never falter. And Jimmy, my stepbrother, who was snatched from us far too early, fond memories of us dancing and playing records.

I would also like to thank the following for their support and friendship over the years: Phil Williams, a great pal and a true friend, and for that I am very grateful; my good mate Andy Parker, thank you for being there; Charlie Gidley my karate coach and more importantly, a great friend and mentor; my good friend, Mike Craig, who filmed and supported my work without moaning or complaining; and Mark Orminston for your kind help with my logo and website.

Finally, I am grateful for the memories I have of the late Ms Whitney Houston. She was a joy to work with, a pleasure to meet, and a fantastic artist.

# INTRODUCTION

This book has taken over ten years to put together. At first, I was just drafting my thoughts about some of the work I'd done over the years, lots of scribbles during many hours sat on a beach reflecting on my life.

I come from a background of hard times. Raised by a single parent on a tough council estate, I was a person of low self-esteem, who went on to become World Karate Champion, and one of only a small number to achieve the rank of 8th Dan Black Belt.

I hope it gives you an insight into a person who came from nothing, who worked hard to get to the pinnacle of my sport, and someone who became a highly respected and experienced bodyguard to some of the most famous people in the world.

Writing this has made me aware of what I have actually done and achieved in my life. I hope my story inspires you to follow your dreams. To realise that no matter who you are, or where you come from - anything is possible.

**Can a man change his stars? Can it be done?
Yes, if he believes enough a man can do anything.**

# PREFACE

The book is split into a number of areas of my life: my history in karate; getting into bodyguarding and close protection; you will get to meet a few of my many clients and the people I have protected over the years; and a look at the training I've developed and delivered to over two-thousand students.

It also brings a reality to the security industry and offers guidance to aspiring bodyguards and security professionals. What to aim for, and how to be a success in this multi-million-pound industry.

I have tried to recreate events, locations and conversations from my memories of them. In order to maintain their anonymity in some instances I have changed the names of individuals and places. In some cases, I have changed certain identifying characteristics and details such as physical properties, occupations and places of residence.

# BODYGUARD – A BRIEF HISTORY

Bodyguards have been around for thousands of years, dating back to the Egyptian times, where they were hired to protect the monarchy and watch over their tombs and monuments. By the time of the 5th Dynasty, kings and nobles began choosing their guards from among the military and ex-military, as well as from foreign nationals such as the Nubian Medjay warriors.

During the era of the Roman Republic the Praetorian Guard, an elite unit of the Imperial Roman army, served as personal bodyguards to the emperors and high-ranking officials such as senators and provincial governors. After the republic's transition into the Roman Empire, the first emperor, Augustus, founded the Guard as his personal security detail.

In premodern Japan the samurai, or bushi, were sworn to protect and kill for the warlord or Shogun. The samurai used a range of weapons such as bows and arrows, spears and guns, but their main weapon and symbol was the sword. The samurai led their lives according to the ethic code of bushido, 'the way of the warrior', which stressed concepts such as loyalty to one's master, self-discipline and respectful behaviour. The samurai way was to think of life as a cherry blossom, brief and perfect in life, but glorious in death.

Today the Pontifical Swiss Guard is responsible for guarding the Pope. The Swiss Guard, which was established in 1506 by Pope Julius II, serves as the de facto military of the Vatican City and is among the oldest military units in continuous operation.

Their dress uniform is a blue, red, orange and yellow jumpsuit with a distinctly Renaissance appearance. A popular misconception is that they were designed by Michelangelo, but that is not true. Their working uniform is more functional, consisting of blue coveralls with a black beret. Both the dress and working uniforms are worn by the guards when on duty in the Vatican City and are readily identifiable.

The Swiss Guard recruits must be unmarried Swiss Catholic males between 19 and 30 years of age who have completed basic training with the Swiss Armed

Forces. They are equipped with traditional weapons, such as the halberd, as well as with modern firearms.

Since the 13 May 1981 assassination attempt on Pope John Paul II, by the Turkish assassin Mehmet Ali Agca, a much stronger emphasis has been placed on the guard's functional, non-ceremonial roles. This has included extended training in unarmed combat and the issue of Sig Sauer pistols and Heckler & Koch submachine guns.

Those are just a small example of the many different groups that have protected people and property over the years. Throughout this book I will explain how I became one of the UK's most respected bodyguards who protected stars from the world of sport and entertainment, safeguarded members of international organisations, and advised and trained government agencies, corporations and the military.

But firstly, let me tell you about my karate journey - one that took me from the tough streets of Middleton in Manchester to become one of the highest graded karateka and World Open Karate Champion. A journey that changed my life, shaped the person I became, and one which made this book possible.

# CHAPTER 1

## TOUGH BEGININNGS

I was born in Middleton in North Manchester on the 5th of August 1960, the third child of Eric and Dorothy Moulton, and brother to my two older sisters, Diane and Elaine. We lived in Lorton Close on the Langley council estate. It was quite a hard estate, and from a young age I grew up around bullies, sadly many of who were supposed to be my friends. I remember many times being left by my mum with people that I thought were friends, but as soon as she'd gone out the door, it would open and gangs of lads and girls would come in the house.

My father, who was a van driver for Kodak, died when I was only nine years of age. I can't remember a great deal about him, apart from he always looked very smart, and never stopped messing about with his car. But I do have some fond memories spending many a happy day in his van while he took deliveries to Blackpool and Southport.

After he passed away, my mum god bless her, had a number of encounters with other men. She never worked, but looked after the family home, and was a good woman at heart. But she didn't really show a great deal of affection towards me.

I was allowed to do my own thing and left to fend for myself. That's when the bullying started and never really stopped. I was subjected to beatings and humiliating incidents. They'd knock me off my bike and call me really bad names – all of which sounds petty, but when it came from so called friends, it hurt.

I remember on one occasion when my mum had gone out there was banging on the doors and windows. My friend at the time told me to let them in. I didn't, and the next thing they'd broken a window and set fire to the curtains.

That sort of thing went on for some time, and that was when I decided I had to protect myself and my family. By a stroke of good fortune or perhaps fate, I was given a book called *How to learn Karate*, by my mate Neil Fagan.

The book inspired me, and I was determined to learn karate, but I couldn't afford to go to the classes, so I built my own punch bag frames and striking boards out of plywood. I improvised as best I could, even making my own set of nunchakus from my mum's brush stale – I'd cut it into two pieces, put a screw in the middle with some chain, and there it was, my very own nunchakus. Funnily my mum never saw the funny side of it - going to get the brush only to find half a handle – and more often than not I'd get it across the backside. My other training aid was a tennis ball on a piece of string in the outhouse. I would jab and kick it for hours, but as you could imagine, the noise got irritating and that was very quickly banned.

At this time, I had nobody to bounce ideas off, or talk about the problems that I had or was going through with the bullying. But I was focused on one thing and that was learning to look after myself. I first learnt how to stretch and kick my own height - which was next to nothing. But the bullies saw this, and soon started to give me a wide berth. At the time karate was not known apart from the television programme Kung Fu starring David Carradine.

Learning the skills out of a book was not the best way but it served a purpose, and eventually, just after my eleventh birthday, I was introduced to a karate class.

I trained three nights a week, but I had to work to pay for my lessons because my mum couldn't afford to help me. My mate Neil Fagan and I would do jobs around the dojo, which included stripping the floorboards to be re-varnished, and that was how I managed to pay for the lessons.

But the jobs at the dojo soon became a convenient excuse for not going to school. In fact, it got to the stage where I never went at all. My mum would write a note and then I would keep one back, but eventually we were found out by Neil's dad, who didn't take kindly. Neil got the belt and I was chased around the house. Then the school's truant officer, Mr Parker, turned up at the dojo which was in Broad Street in Middleton. The instructors at the time were Jeff Parker, a very slight guy, but a fantastic kicker, and Jeff Corbishly, who was very stocky. My favourite however, was Maggie Chan, who was only small but an awesome karateka and brilliant with weapons. Maggie said I must go to school and the fear of me not being able to train made me attend - not all the time, but more than I did.

I had found my passion in life and something to hold onto. When I first started karate there was a great deal of clubs around, and mostly everything was focused on the great Bruce Lee, who like many others, was an inspiration to me.

When I didn't train at the club, I trained at home. I built my own striking boards and punchbag out of an old post bag. There was no internet or YouTube in those days, so basically it was about reading books and watching any films you could get to see. Not being eighteen years old was an issue with getting to the cinema, but there was always a way around that!

After my father had passed away money was scarce. My mum didn't work, and apart from the cash she got from having lodgers in the house, there wasn't much left for me. My older sister Elaine bought my first karate suit, which is known as a gi. She took me to Hurley's in Manchester, it was not the one I wanted – it was a thin flimsy thing – but at least I had my own one.

Because we were classed as a one parent family I was given free school dinners, and vouchers to buy my school uniform. This was something I hated, all my friends had brogues with the tips or Dr Martin boots, and I had horrible pretend leather shoes, which always split. I remember quite vividly using Airfix glue to seal them together, and then putting them under the couch leg to make them stick, which worked for a while before they started to split again. Of course, this was okay during the summer, but in the winter time I often had to revert to Plan B, which was wearing plastic bags inside my shoes to keep my feet dry.

I hated going to school and karate was the only thing I was interested in. Football was the main sport we did during PE, but I detested it. I had the most out of date football kit, a black and white shirt, an old Newcastle United one I think, pale blue shorts, and white plastic boots. All my mates had screw in studs which sounded great on the tarmac, but I had plastic ones, so I used to stick drawing pins in to each stud so they made a sound – until they fell out of course. At one stage I even refused to take part in the training - which wasn't one of my better moves - as I was made to wear shorts that had been dyed pink. I don't think the school would get away with that nowadays. This went on for months until one day the gym teacher called me over.

'Moulton what do you want to do?' he asked.

I said some lads do weight lifting, so why can't I do karate? A simple question, and to my surprise he agreed.

Soon there were six of us all training together. Myself and Neil Fagan, the twins Mark and Martin Wright, a lad called Pete King and my best mate at the time Steve Green. We ended up going to different karate classes that were springing up in the area, and as you can imagine, we had a few scraps around the various dojos. But above all else, we showed each other respect even though we were from different classes – it was the karate that held us all together.

At that time, it would have been very easy for me to turn to the wrong side and use my karate skills for the wrong reasons. I was challenged many times in certain ways but my focus and discipline kept me on the right path. However, there were many times when I got into street fights, some I won and some I didn't fare so well – I'll never say I lost – I just learnt!

# CHAPTER 2

## BLACK BELT AND ENGLAND

After leaving school I continued to practice karate. I developed my skills and became recognised as an exponent of martial arts - building up karate classes around the area. I also became a member of the England Shukokai Karate Union (SKU) squad, something I achieved before I'd gained my black belt.

I was on the England SKU squad from 1980 to 1984. I gained my place at the grade of $4^{th}$ kyu, which is purple belt, having had to compete for my spot against a $2^{nd}$ Dan black belt. He made a little bit of a mess of my face, but my old friend, and then instructor, Neil Fagan shouted at me from the edge to get on with it, and within a very short space of time I had beaten a higher grade to get my England place.

On the squad selection there was about sixty of us there for over four hours of very hard training. It started with a run, then the warm ups, and then onto line and pair work – they were hard sessions and we suffered our share of knocks, bumps and bruises. Once we completed those sessions we went into sparring, which again were full on, semi contact - controlled to head and face at times - but more or less full contact to the body.

Then we were split into two sections – one section of newbies and the other were old school - but each had to fight for their place. At the helm was Sensei Stan Knighton the head coach of the SKU squad, a big guy with a great presence. We had to compete against higher grades to gain that coveted spot, it was strange for them to see a lower grade compete, but as the saying goes - never judge a book by its cover. As a 4th kyu I had beaten a 2nd Dan - taken a few belts in the process - but I had made the England squad.

When I first started karate, my aim was to get a black belt. Over the years I had worked hard to get through the grades, but before I could go for the black belt there was a certain criteria that had to be met. I had to be at least a qualified judge to enter as a grade, so I had to attend a referee and judge's course. These were held at the University of Manchester Institute of Science and Technology (UMIST). I went to the course with my old mate Pete Ringland. Pete was a great pal and very sharp, his problem was his control, which he admitted himself wasn't good.

As a course we had to demonstrate how to control a fight. Pete was brought in because he would always belt someone in the mouth or nose and get disqualified. After a gruelling five hours, two of which were speaking in Japanese, I managed to pass. The following day, Neil Fagan came and picked me up to go teaching, and said 'Oh by the way you have missed the ref's course so you can't grade'. With a smile I passed him my certificate and the look on his face was priceless.

When I started training for my black belt I trained every day. Even after a night out I would practise my kata on the old Bowlee airfield with my stepbrother Jimmy Haycock – thinking about it now we must have looked like a pair of loonies.

I trained very hard, we were at it every night and Saturday and Sunday afternoons we concentrated on sparring. Every day I pedalled my bike up and down a hill on Broad Street in Middleton – it was one of the steepest hills in the area. I remember being in Corfu on holiday and practicing my katas on the beach every morning, and while I was at work I practiced them in the warehouse when it was quiet.

On the weekend of my blackbelt grading, I went back to the UMIST. The gradings were held on the top floor of the YMCA. It started on the Friday night with kata and basics, then up to 4 pm on the Saturday we did combinations, sparring and pad work, and Saturday night we graded. There were fifteen students going for the black belt.

When it came time to grade my gi was soaking wet from the sweat, I wanted to look my best but didn't have a spare one. Neil Fagan, who was one of the grading instructors, told me not to worry as he would lend me his Tokido gi, so thinking I was all sorted out, I started to focus on what I had to do. But as the time got closer I was dealt a blow. Neil came up to me with the gi, but not the one I was expecting, instead it was one that was ripped all down the side. There I was preparing for one of the most important moments in karate, and I'd been let down my mate. But rather than moan about it, I just sat quietly in the corner of the room. I focused on passing the grading, which in those days, the line ups were hard - the instructors on the panel were 4th Dans and above.

Our grading was set for 6.30 pm and we were to be graded by Roy Stanhope 5th Dan, who was the Great Britain coach and Stan Knighton 5thDan, the England Team Manager. Nervously we lined up and started with combinations, then moved on to pad work, and finished off with kata. The final aspect was sparring or

Ippon Kumite competition. We fought hard, I was a lightweight, but always very fast with my left lead leg and sweeps.

When the grading finished you weren't told your level, only if you had passed or failed. Out of the fifteen students that started only seven passed. I gained the highest mark, my instructor came over to me and said 'well done, but your blocks were too high'. A point that stuck in mind for some time. After it was over we all went to Chinatown for a meal before going home to share the news.

So, in 1982, about twelve years after Neil Fagan had given me the book: *How to learn Karate* - I had gained my black belt.


During that period, I fought in a lot of competitions including the Quest for Champions, which was one of the very first continuous sparring contests. It was held in the CIS building in Manchester and I faired quite well including the team kata. The Quest for Champions was run by the late Danny Connor, a great man, who owned the famous martial arts shop, Oriental World. Although it was a karate competition they had introduced the freestyle aspect of the sport, and needless to say there were plenty of knocks and bumps throughout the competition.

Over time I had gained a number of titles including runner up in the SKU National Championships. I still remember that feeling before going on the mat - sometimes against lads a lot bigger than myself - focus was always in the front of my mind.

This picture is of me delivering one of my favourite kicks - a reverse hook kick. This was published in Combat Magazine.

# CHAPTER 3

## BEATING THE BULLIES

In my home town of Middleton, I began building a number of karate classes. We visited schools in the area, performed demonstrations, and built up quite a good following, which at times was over one hundred students. One of my first classes was at the place where it began back in 1970 - Springvale Social Centre.

My classes became very popular and attracted students from all ages. My main focus was on teaching the discipline of traditional karate.

As I mentioned earlier, I was bullied by a lot of people when I was young, and one karate related occasion still sticks in my mind. I had few friends at school, so the ones I did have meant a lot to me. There were a few who were very quiet, not scrappers or troublesome. Then one day a new lad turned up at school and everyone flocked around him. Because of the karate he befriended me, we trained together, did bits of sparring and became quite pally.

Anyway, one day I was walking home from school, I was with the lad, who was living in a foster home at the time, and a pal of mine called Vic Tyson. The three of us were walking along fine until we got to the road where the lad lived, and then, for no reason, he turned to Vic and head butted him in the face and sent him flying.

I said 'what the f**k are you doing?'

He turned around and said that Vic was not a mate and that I didn't like him, then the clown tried to headbutt me too. But he got a little shock himself and we ended up in a scuffle. As we parted the pain in my face wasn't a problem, it was the fact I thought he was a pal that bothered me more than anything.

Many years later I was teaching karate and got a phone call - the caller said, 'do you remember me?' and of course it was him.

'I certainly do,' I replied.

'Can I come training with you?' he asked.

'Of course, you can,' I said.

Now I didn't know this at the time, but apparently, he had served a little time after getting in trouble with police. He turned up with a brown belt around his waist, I never mentioned his conduct from years before, and started to train him. All was fine until one day while sparring he turned to me and said, 'come on hero let's see what you've got', and started trying his best to hurt me. Well at that time I was renowned for my hard left mawashi-geris and sweeps, and it would have been easy for me just to hurt him. But I kept my focus and discipline, swept him countless times and floored him a number of left roundhouse kicks.

His attitude towards me changed after this, but then he started on the police officers who trained with me, on one occasion splitting my good mate's lip. Again, this resulted in me having to discipline him, and after a few hard lessons he apologised to them.

Sadly, he was a bit of a repeat offender type, and really had a hang up with the police. The final straw came when he rocked up at the club with a plaster cast on his arm saying he had got into a fight. I told him he could train but not spar, but he took it upon himself to start sparring with a police officer and laid into him really bad.

Bullies prey on people's vulnerabilities, and he had done it to me in the past, something I had always hated. I addressed the situation by speaking to the police officer he'd hurt, and then told him there was no more to be said, and he'd have to leave the club. He had wanted to demonstrate his prowess, but had failed miserably. I had embarrassed him and shown the weak person that he was. As he left I said to him, 'Remember Vic Tyson from years ago? He couldn't fight you then and that was for him'.

This picture was taken sixteen years later, in 1986 – it was me going back to my roots.

Over the years I kept in touch with a few mates from the early days. Neil Fagan, who I have mentioned was one, and Pete King was another. Pete, who was the cock of the school, became one of my students, and was a really funny lad. On one competition, the Nationals at Belle Vue in Manchester, a lad called Graham Cleworth was fighting. Now Pete was known for his outbursts, and

41

although the guy wasn't getting the better of Graham, he was giving him the run around, and kept pushing the fingers from his open hand in Graham's face.

Having seen enough, Pete shouted from the edge of the mat 'grab his fingers and snap them off!'. Well, they stopped the fight and the head judge, who was Dave Warburton 4th Dan at the time, came over to Pete and spoke to him very quietly.

Wanting to find out what he'd said I went over to a sheepish looking Pete and asked him.

'If I open my mouth one more time he'll ban me from the competition' he said before adding 'and I thought he was coming over to ask me for advice!'

We entered many competitions over the years and faired very well, we fought very hard and suffered many injuries. On one occasion I was competing in the Lancashire Opens, fighting as normal in the open weights. I came across this guy who was a great deal taller than me, we exchanged a chat and we ended up fighting each other on the mat. I will never forget this one - he was leaving the UK to go and live in Australia the following day, so he wanted to make it a good finish. We fought for six points and I was beating him hands down. I was leading 4-0 when he caught me with a great roundhouse kick. I thought he'd broke my back, in fact I found out later that he'd broken two ribs. I had thirty seconds to last out and couldn't get my breath. But I dug in and actually swept him that hard that both his legs left the ground and he landed with a thump on the floor. I think it was the pain that drove me on, but it didn't finish there as we ended up meeting once more in the team event. I fought him again, with all his pals shouting 'go for his ribs'. I must admit, the thought of getting belted again did spur me on, and after what seemed to be the longest three minutes, we ended up winning the team and individuals.

# CHAPTER 4

## RECORD BREAKER

My knowledge and experience in the martial arts have been put to good use not only by teaching students, but completing several charity events. One of which was in 1996, when I broke 875 roof tiles in 75 seconds, to raise money for children in Bosnia and Croatia.

I also knew the world record for tile breaking was 980 concrete tiles in 90 seconds, so I decided to attempt to break it and raise money for another charity. At the time the children's television programme, Blue Peter, were raising funds for people suffering from leprosy. So, I decided to do it for them.

I spoke to two local firms: Asphaltic Roofing Supplies, who agreed to supply the tiles; and Lewis Brothers who gave bricks to prop them on. I arranged for them to be dropped off at the venue, which was the back yard of St. Peter's Hall, on Townley Street, Middleton. I unloaded them by myself and wrecked my back in the process. The plan was for me to smash through them with my hands, but on the day of the event I couldn't even bend over. My coach, Charlie Gidly, who also did my physio, laid me down and then stripped the nodules in my muscles, which hurt like hell.

With the tiles all set up, and a crowd of about fifty family and supporters gathered, we were ready to go. I started to plough through them using my feet, and when I got to the last few stacks I smashed them with my hands, but because it was freezing cold there was condensation on the tiles and they'd became a sold block. I still managed to smash through them, but I must admit, it did sting a bit and I ended up with a few splinters in my hands.

But the good news was I had smashed 1025 tiles in 90 seconds and set a new world record. We'd also raised over £200 for charity, which the club sent off to the Blue Peter Leprosy Appeal, along with a video of me breaking the record. We didn't get a mention on the programme, which was a pity, but the local news did and we knew we had achieved something.

The photograph below is from an event I organised for a friend of mine called Diana who was suffering from cancer.

It was Christmas time, she was struggling for money, and was completely unaware of what I was doing. She turned up at the karate club thinking she was part of the class until I announced the real reason, and there were a few tears shed to say the least. I ended up breaking 200 concrete tiles in 30 seconds. We raised a few pounds for her and gave it to her on the night.

I was very proud of my karate classes, which were called the Bushido Karate Centres. We entered many competitions and the students always did very well, we trained hard, and the lessons were very long and varied, never just the traditional classes.

This photograph is me going back to my roots at Springvale Social Club in 1988. It was an inter-club competition, which was also our Christmas event.

Some of the students here went on to become 3rd and 4th dan black belts, the youngest was just 11 years old, again proving you can achieve anything if you work at it. The clubs progressed over the years, and students came and went, but the one thing that I could guarantee was that all my students made gains in kumite (fighting), kata (forms) and achieved their gradings.

I prided myself on being a good instructor. Mathew Rathmill, one of my former students once commented that I was one of the hardest and strictest instructors he ever trained under. And one of my closest friends, Andy Parker, told me a funny story about my reputation. Andy was a police sergeant, and on one occasion he had to attend a hospital to arrest a person. When he arrived, the hospital staff warned him that the person in question was likely to kick off, as he tended to fight with anyone. As Andy waited he heard a commotion and then the guy came flying out. Andy stood his ground and waited for the right opportunity to restrain him. Seeing Andy, the guy became abusive and squared up to him, telling him that he knew karate. But to his surprise Andy said 'so do I'.

'Who is your instructor?' the guy asked.

'Sensei Phil Moulton' Andy's reply

'Oh f**k that! I'll come quietly then, he's a f**king animal and if he trained you I'm not messing with you!' I knew nothing about this until a few years later when Andy was telling my wife Nadia, leaving us in fits of laughter.

# CHAPTER 5

## WORLD CHAMPION

After a bit of a lay off from competing, a competition came along, and guess what, a few of the police officers that I was training gave me a little bit of a dig to do it. The competition was the 1996 World Open All Style Karate Championships.

My focus was now on winning a major event, but I hadn't competed in a major competition since 1984. At the time I had four jobs: building work during the day; any security jobs that I could pick up at night; teaching karate and working in a shop. I was working seven days a week, but cash was never really there - the story of my life, but despite all of that, I still managed to train hard.

When the competition came around I travelled down to Sheffield with a few friends, one being John Weaver, who had trained with me for many years gaining his 3rd dan black belt.

However, my quest to be world champion didn't get off to a good start. The night before I was really ill with flu like symptoms, and on the day of the competition I was full of the flu.

I knew the venue well as it was where I had trained from 1980 until 1984 with the England SKU squad. As the event unfolded all the swish karate gis came out, and I remember sitting there with my woolly jumper on.

It soon came my time to do the kata, which was Seipai. It was something that I had focused on during my training; I had been through it time after time, and despite the flu I gave it everything. I wasn't aware of it at the time, but John told me once I had finished you could have heard a pin drop.

The competition continued and I went through a number of eliminations, until eventually it was all finished. I waited nervously as they announced the results in reverse order. To my surprise, the guy who had won the championship for the past four consecutive years, and who had also been inducted into the Martial Arts Illustrated Hall of Fame, was given second place.

And then they announced first place and it was me! I couldn't believe it, nor could the guy who came second. He came over and congratulated me, and with a grin said 'I wish you'd stayed in retirement'.

Winning the competition was one of the most fantastic achievements of my life. With very little support, I had focused on winning. I'd trained hard, practiced my kata again and again, and been crowned karate World Champion.

1996 World Open Karate Champion

# CHAPTER 6

## BLACK BELT 8th DAN

Having become the 1996 World Champion, I wasn't about to go back into retirement, and over the next few years I went on to compete at the highest level. Below are some of my most notable results on the National, European and World stage:

1999 – European Karate Championships – 2nd & 3rd

2000 – British Karate Championships – 3rd

2002 – World Karate Championship Las Vegas – 4th

2012 – British National Karate Championships – 3rd

The 1999 European Karate Championships:

In 2002 I attended a competition in Las Vegas. The event was the Funakoshi World Karate Championships. It was a Shotokan competition, and although I was Shukokai, I competed in the kata. The organisers were the direct decedents of Gichin Funakoshi, the man known as the 'father of karate'. His grandsons Kenneth and Kevin were there; I got to the finals and during my kata, my wife Nadia saw Kenneth taking photographs of me. I finished in fourth place, a result I was very proud of.

While competing I continued to work my way up the dan grades, which wasn't easy as there is a time limit of two years from 1st Dan to 2$^{nd}$ Dan, three years for 3$^{rd}$ Dan, and so on. In 2005 I obtained my 7$^{th}$ Dan black belt after being graded by Sensei Charles Gidley, 7$^{th}$ Dan, and head of TBSKA.

This is me receiving my 7$^{th}$ Dan certificate at the Lowry Hotel. Sensei Gidley was from the old school of Shotokan, the bloke in the background is my brother-in-law, who enjoyed getting into people's photographs.

In 2013, eight years later, I graded for, and was awarded my 8th Dan black belt again by Sensei Charles Gidley 9th Dan.

Throughout those years I had to attend many courses and took referee exams. The last competition I entered was the British National Opens. Sensei Gidley, having a good sense of humour, asked me what I was doing at the weekend?

I said, 'Nothing.'

He asked, 'Do you fancy coming to a competition on Sunday? There's a veterans kata, do you fancy it?'

I agreed to go, Nadia came with me, and when we turned up at the event all the instructors were stood there.

'Where are the veterans?' I asked, sensing something wasn't right.

'There isn't any!' they replied.

I had been set up. I hadn't practised any kata for a long time, and I was up against a group of young 2nd, 3rd and 4th Dans.

The competition started and I waited in the line-up with the other thirty competitors. When it was my turn I did my first kata. After the first round some people were eliminated, and when it was my turn again, I did my second kata. During competitions I never really notice what is happening around me as my focus is on performing to the best of my ability. This was the case in the second round, and while I was doing my kata the hall went totally quiet - I didn't notice it, but my wife Nadia did. She was watching with a girl from the England team, who was about eighteen years old. After my performance she told Nadia that was the standard she would love to get to. I did my third kata and then progressed to the final. Despite a lack of training, and competing against much younger competitors, I came third and I was very happy.

With my 8th Dan certificate

# CHAPTER 7

## BECOMING A BODYGUARD

One of the first 'bodyguarding' jobs that I did was looking after my mum, god bless her. With my father passing away early in her life, my mum had a number of encounters with other men, even if it was frowned upon in those days. She was never short of money, but that was something that I never felt the benefit of, even though she was always lending cash to others.

In 1977 she met her new husband, Larry. There was always a great deal of jealousy in the close where we lived. On the day of their wedding a lady who she had loaned money to, decided to sit herself on the edge of the square with a bucket of horse manure to throw at her as she got into the wedding car.

At the time I was not even sixteen years old, and the thought of this infuriated me, ok my mum wasn't an angel, but she did help others, including that woman. As the wedding car drew up I went out and told the driver to reverse up the square to the front door. As my mum got into the car, the people who had gathered started jeering at her. I then walked alongside it until it got to the road, jumped in and we drove off – my first experience of escorting a VIP!

At the church I was there to open the car door and basically took the lead for the wedding – not bad for a sixteen-year-old. After the happy event we returned home to find the house windows smashed and the curtains set on fire again. Outside there was a large group, which were mostly lads that I knew. They started jeering again, so I confronted them; asking why they were doing what they were doing, the answer was not what I expected. 'We're not and never have been your mates, and who do you think you are anyway? You're a nothing and so is your mum,' they said. Well there was a little bit of scuffle, let's call it handbags at dawn, but it made me realise then that friends can be very fickle, which is something that has resounded throughout my life.

During the late 70's in Manchester there was rivalry between ice cream vans. On the Langley estate where I lived there were two or three vans going around, and my mate Steve Saunders drove one of them.

Steve was a nice lad; he loved the Beatles, but was nothing to look at, and actually lived at our house as a lodger, my mum knew his father, and we were sort of 'cousins'. At the time there was a lot of attacks on the vans, sometimes with baseball bats, and the drivers and sellers were being intimidated. I hadn't witnessed it myself, but Steve asked me if I'd keep him company while he was doing his rounds.

We travelled around in his van, he couldn't afford to pay me, but gave me free ice cream, and I was just happy to be with him. I did this for a few weeks, and in my mind, I was just there to keep him company and nothing more. But after a while it started to interfere with my karate training so I knocked it on the head. It was only years later that I found out the real reason why he wanted me with him, not for company, but having me there as a presence because I knew karate!

I was teaching karate six days a week for my old friend and instructor, Neil Fagan, who had become a bit negative and started to hold me back on my grades. We trained hard and sparred even harder. I had built a good reputation for my sparring and katas, and many of my students followed me to other classes.

It was at that time that I crossed paths with a student who was a senior member of the Greater Manchester Police's Serious Crime Unit. After teaching him for a number of years he said that I would make a good minder. I took on board what he said and started to look into bodyguarding. But as usual the problem I had was the lack of funds to pay for the training courses that I would need to break into the market. But I was determined, and it was my desire to teach others how to look after themselves, and to protect people who were being bullied or intimidated.

I was still doing four jobs and tried everything to get a break, including contacting people in America. I even remember contacting The Hollywood Reporter magazine to offer my services and even placed an advertisement in it, but sadly no response. I also contacted my karate contacts in the US and got quite a good response, they even invited me over, but again the lack of money prevented me from going.

Eventually I got a break and attended a Close Protection (CP) course in 1992 that was being run by a chap I knew. But despite having the CP qualification it started to feel that I was going around in circles. The companies wanted you to pay thousands of pounds to go on courses so that you could 'get work', but more often than not the jobs never happened.

Over the years I remember going for many interviews at a lot of different places. I chased my dreams, phoning people day and night, only to be told by most that they didn't need such services. On one occasion I contacted a dance company in London. After numerous telephone conversations I eventually travelled down to meet them. When I got to London I met a lady called Susan Bruce, and found out that the company shared offices with a charity called the Rainforest Foundation, which had been founded by the singer, Sting. At one point there was talk of introducing me to Sting's charity but it never happened either.

Despite the disappointments I persevered and then I came across a lady who I never met, but owe a great deal to. Her name was Vicky Standeven and she was highly regarded in the TV industry. She first contacted me in the late 1990's to do a little bit of security work on a TV set. I ended up doing quite a few jobs for her including one on a documentary about a lady who had stood up to local gangsters, and actually had a loaded gun put in her face. The lady was awarded the Pride of Britain award by the late Cilla Black, and we were filming a documentary about her on the local estate.

The film crew started to attract a little attention from the locals, and at the time we had two police officers with us. As the morning progressed I noticed a car driving up and down the road, at first there was only one person in it, then it became two, and soon there were three. I spoke with the police officers, and they radioed through as they passed again. The car was pulled over at the bottom of road, and all the occupants were detained. I don't know if they were charged but they were quickly locked up, the film crew knew nothing about it until the producer informed them. The lady was a great person, very courageous and really deserved the award.

Not all the jobs were dangerous; I did another one for Vicky which was for a TV documentary called 'Hens and Stags'. It was about a group of hen and stag parties. Mine was a hen party from a council estate in Liverpool who were going to Blackpool for the night. They were visiting a number of clubs and pubs, so I contacted the door staff to help them gain safe and quick entry. We visited one club which was very similar to the old TV show 'It Ain't Half Hot Mum', and because we were filming there was quite a few people ducking down. I found the night quite funny, and there were no problems until the end of the night, when a group of lads tried to get in on the action on the bus. A harsh word without getting irate worked, and they even apologised. I find that if you speak to people with respect, you'll get the same back.

Because of my skills and reputation, I was soon accepted into some of the bodyguarding groups that were doing the circuit. But I was still doing four jobs and decided that one would have to go. Although it brought in the most money, I chose the building work, as it was the one that was stopping me from training and helping others, and doing my dream job.

One of the groups I was with specialised in providing security for royalty from the Middle East. After I gained their trust I was put forward to be the principle guard for the son of His Royal Highness Prince Fiasal, the Crown Prince of Saudi Arabia. This was the break I was looking for, but unfortunately the break-up of my marriage at that time, stopped me from taking the job.

However, after a short period on my own I met Nadia, the person who would give me more strength than I could ever imagine. Three months after meeting her we were engaged, and she became my best mate, and wife.

From the beginning she was behind me and encouraged me to achieve my dream. I gave up a job as a safety trainer, and another as a plain clothes investigator, to set up my dream job. Living on nothing and chasing everything, I provided security for clients that was difficult to beat. I achieved this with very little money, but a lot of belief in what I was doing.

# CHAPTER 8

## I'LL BE WATCHING YOU

In 1998, which seemed to be a great year for me, I was working as a lone close protection officer (CPO) for a corporate client who'd had a number of threats against him. It was not business or anything glamorous, basically he'd been caught messing around with another man's wife. The interesting thing about the job was that the guy who was making the threats was a former CPO in the Armed Forces. My job was to shadow the client and carry out covert protection. As I say nothing glamorous but it did lead into something that certainly was.

Whitney Houston, one of the world's most famous singers at that time, was on a ten-date tour of Europe, including a concert in Manchester. I knew this because a contact of mine had already told me they wanted to use me while she was in Manchester. I had declined it as I was already guarding the corporate client. However, a chap called John May contacted me and asked if I could meet him at the Malmaison hotel in Manchester. I asked what for, but he just laughed and asked me to come down. When I got there I was met in the hotel bar by John and two police officers. John explained that the four-day job was very sensitive and asked me to take it, which I did. Essentially, I was to make sure there was no issues between Whitney and her husband, the R&B singer, Bobby Brown!

Whitney was very a pleasant person, with a great personality. All the time I was with her I only saw her personal security team, that had come with her from the US, a handful of times. Something which I found quite odd. I spoke with her on a number of occasions, mostly about music, but she never once mentioned the real reason why I was there.

One night after the concert had finished, and she was back in the hotel, her bedroom door opened and she asked me if I enjoyed gospel music. I said I did, and so she spent the next sixty-minutes singing to warm her voice down – it felt like my own personal concert.

Over the four days my role was to maintain the security of her and her daughter. Her husband was known to be quite a character and we did end up having a little bit of a confrontation on the final night. This was caused by his presence on Whitney's floor and his demands to see her. He was very aggressive and tried to intimidate me - which didn't work. The noise had got quite loud, and I was surprised that Whitney's personal security team where nowhere to be seen. We continued our loud discussion for a number of minutes, and then he became very irate because he couldn't get past me. It took another five minutes or so before one of her security team came out, and by that time Bobby Brown was in my face, spitting and giving me the 'do I know who I am?' attitude – a silly question really!

I advised her team member to remove him, otherwise I would, and at that point Whitney came out just as Bobby was being moved off the floor. She came over to me a short time later and apologized for his actions.

One thing I don't do is slate a VIP or a member of their group unless I deem its right to do so. In this case I believe her security team should have been more forceful and controlled the situation better, but sometimes guarding a high-profile person can lead to complacency. This seems to be a problem with some security operatives and bodyguards who look after bands or famous people. Some take advantage of their new-found stardom and think they are more important than the clients they look after.

# I'LL BE WATCHING YOU

POP diva Whitney Houston's very own bodyguard is alive and well and living in Castleton. Personal protection officer Philip Moulton would not claim to have the superstar looks or style of Kevin Costner, her co-star in the film 'The Bodyguard', but he can boast that the glamorous international singer gave him a personal impromptu concert in her Manchester hotel suite.

"It was brilliant. I was escorting her and her children around while she was on tour. We'd got back to the hotel room and she made some comment about it being quiet and put the radio on. Then she began singing along at the top of her voice. It was amazing. It went on for quite a while, a private performance just for me!" said Phil.

"She was lovely to work for, no problems at all."

But it isn't always easy dealing with the various temperaments of the rich and famous.

One top British rock singer who shall remain nameless became very annoyed when Phil refused to take him to the Armani shop in Manchester.

"It was 10 in the morning, we were still in his hotel suite in Manchester and his plane was due to leave an hour later. He became quite insistent that he was going to Armani to choose a shirt. I had to become equally insistent and say 'I'm sorry sir you haven't got time'.

"He was not at all pleased and became quite awkward and moody. Eventually he saw sense and at the airport he thanked me for getting him there on time and acknowledged he'd been out of order."

This down-to-earth 39-year-old father of two has a string of anecdotes about the rich and famous gathered in the 20 years he has been chauffeuring and providing protection and security services to VIPs.

He is no stranger to the foibles of the likes of Tina Turner, Celine Dion, Tom Jones and Bryan Adams. He has even looked after top politicians and foreign royalty. Stars can be very demanding and their exalted positions means they are used to their every wish being granted – and pronto. Clients can expect him to drop everything day or night to suit their needs.

"I looked after Bryan Adams when he came to the Manchester Evening News Arena. It was hard work because he runs everywhere, literally. You have to run everywhere too with him, so it was just as well I'm fairly fit. He also hates having security staff around, but at the end of my time with him he was very nice and appreciative," said Phil loyally.

Always the truly discreet professional, tales of the top people's tantrums are hard to prise from him.

"I know that not everyone in my profession remains tight-lipped but I think spilling the beans is very unprofessional. I make a point of never asking to have my photograph taken with them. I am there to minimise the hassle they get, not add to it. Luckily, most of the people I've worked for have been great with me," he says.

He has fond memories of the visit of the legendary footballer Pele to Manchester for the opening of Manchester United's football museum.

"He was here for four days and I collected him from the airport and went everywhere with him, the main job being to make sure that he was not hassled or hurt by over-enthusiastic fans.

"He is a lovely man, but it was hard work for two reasons. One, the Spice Girls were in town and everywhere we went in *continued on page 12*

A feature article about when I looked after Whitney.

# CHAPTER 9

## TRUST

Working in many areas, building up clients, and gaining trust is a big factor in the security industry, especially if you don't have a military or police background.

Because of the trust that I had gained from many clients, I was asked to do a number of security and close protection jobs, one of which included driving for a French government minister for four days. While in the UK he had his own French police officer with him, my job was to be his driver. I ensured that all the routes were checked, and his car was searched – something I did myself. We had police outriders throughout the task and to be quite honest it was more fun than a job. We have to wear many hats in this business, but it's good to know your limits.

Another short job I did was for the singer Errol Brown, from the soul band, Hot Chocolate. The job involved myself and a driver, and our task was to pick Errol up from a hotel in Manchester and take him to the airport to catch his flight. There had been issues in the past with autograph hunters harassing Errol, so with that in mind, my good friend Phil Williams had hired me to escort him to the airport. The driver who was with me was a nice guy called Bill. He worked for a local company, and although I hadn't used his services before, I gave him a shot.

We met Errol in the hotel lobby, and while Bill took his luggage to the car, he told me he wanted to go to a shop to pick up a new shirt. Now time was not on our side, the flight was early in the morning so traffic was an issue. Now this is where some security people fall foul as there is normally two options to take:

Option 1 - Let the VIP do what they want and risk missing the flight. Plus, the issue of additional cost and stress of getting another one; or the knock-on effects such as having to reschedule a TV appearance or show. All of which could result in the company losing that and future jobs.

or

Option 2 - Advise the VIP accordingly of the above; stand your ground and advise the client or company of your actions.

I took Option 2 and advised him he couldn't go shopping due to time and traffic issues. Well a few harsh words and looks followed, but I didn't budge and we soon got on our way to the airport. As we got into the car, Bill had the music on, and he was playing the Hot Chocolate song 'You Sexy Thing'. As Errol climbed into the back of the car Bill turned to him and said 'Hey, Errol, I remember this the first time around!'

Well he gave him a look that said it all, and if the seat could have opened up for me, I would have crawled inside it!

We got him to Manchester Airport without any issues and I escorted him to customs, where I handed him over to an escort. He thanked me, and then said 'Don't use that driver again!' I never told Bill, bless him.


While I was head of security at a the Malmaison hotel I got a call to say that Roger Taylor, the drummer from Queen was in the hotel, and that he was planning to go to a local night club.

Now this wasn't my job, but I took it on because I knew that the club was in a busy part of town with lots of clubs and bars. And as it was a Saturday night they'd be busy and full of drunks.

I introduced myself to Roger and asked if he had any security with him, to which he replied 'No, I have my manager, PA and driver.'

I told him about the area that they were going to and asked if I could set up safe travel for him and his group. His PA asked if it was that bad, which I replied it can be and it's going to be busy.

Gilly Morgan, a good friend of mine, was head of security at the venue. Gilly is a nice guy with a good presence, I called him and asked who was on the door, luckily, he said it was him. I told him I was bringing over a VIP and asked him to arrange a clear route in.

We walked through the area, there were a lot of people, many of who were drunk. We got to one point where there had been a fight, and as we walked passed a young guy was sat covered in blood. Roger turned to me with a look of shock on his face and I said, 'let's just keep going'.

I phoned ahead and spoke to Gilly who got his staff out the front and cleared the area - it was like the parting of the Red Sea. Needless to say, Roger was very happy, and actually said to me 'You are the man, aren't you!'

I handed him over to the venue staff, and organised the same security for him to get back. Later that night he returned safely to the hotel, and thanked me again.

I was tasked by the Malmaison many times to look after VIPs, everyone from movie stars to opera singers. On one job I had to drive and look after the actor and singer, Sir Michael Crawford. This was my first job for a very large film and music company so it had to be done right. I got the call and had to pick him up at Newcastle Airport.

I contacted the airport and was put through to the security department, this was in the late 90s, so there was a lot of freedom if you went through the correct channels. I picked him up at the airport and he asked if I had done a recce, and I told him that I had.

I took him to a number of venues in and around Newcastle, and then the following day to Manchester. Travelling to Manchester we got caught short when the petrol warning light came on halfway across the Pennines. I had to slip off the road into a small town to fill up, which was frowned upon. I must admit that was not one of my favourite jobs.

There was another occasion when I was tasked by a company who Vicky Standeven had recommended me to. The job was to escort the actor Darren Day to a theatre where he was due to perform. When I checked his flight, I found it was delayed and contacted the client to let them know. It turned out that the actor had to be on stage for curtain call. I contacted Manchester Airport through my network and spoke to a lady who had helped me before on another job. The flight eventually took off from its location and when it arrived at Manchester the airport arranged for Darren to be brought to the front of the plane and escorted through customs directly to me. I got him to the theatre on time and received a great reference from the client.

Over the years I have attended a lot of work-related interviews, travelled around the UK and overseas, and have come across some good and some very bad jobs.

On one occasion I got a call from a private security company that I had previously had an interview with. They asked me to travel to London that day, which I did. I arrived at Claridge's, the five-star hotel in Mayfair, and was taken to the Operations Room.

I was told that my job was to be on the door for a high-profile VIP. I asked who, and they told me, without going into detail he was a member of Saudi Royal Family. It turned out to be His Royal Highness Crown Prince Faisal. I asked for the risk and threat assessments, but was told that I didn't need them, 'just stop anyone getting into the room without authorisation' I was told - at which point my alarm bells started ringing.

But I was down there, so I had to make it work. The Crown Prince and his party left the hotel, so basically, I became the resident security team. I didn't mind, but as the night drew on I had no contact on the radio and none from the hotel, in fact the only contact I had was with a manservant.

One of the lead guys for the private security company I was working for came back to the hotel and told me I would be relieved through the night. I asked him what the deal was, and his response left me stunned: 'Any problems, you can handle them yourself, they are coming back shortly and I'm leaving you to it!'

Before the Crown Prince and his party came back I was greeted by a guy who asked me who I was and if we were the police. I told him we weren't and that we were just a private security company. It turned out that he was the head of security for the hotel. By that time, I had been on post for seven hours with no relief, and was desperate for the loo. We got chatting and I briefed him on what I knew and then asked if he knew anything about the Crown Prince's visit or the security arrangements. I wasn't surprised when he told me he didn't.

I hadn't been told, but I knew from talking to the lead guy from the private security company, that there were other members of the security team in other locations in the hotel. When the Crown Prince and his party arrived back I greeted them, cleared the room, and waited in an area out of the way, but within earshot, if needed. The Crown Prince was surrounded by a number of important looking people and a short time later I was asked to clear the room, which I did, quietly and without any fuss.

After everyone had retired it was getting close to 6am, which meant I had been up and awake nearly twenty-four hours. I was still waiting for my relief, but there was still no sign of it when another guy turned up looking very ashen and pale faced. I asked who he was and he said he was part of the security and like me he hadn't been relieved or had back up either. I told him to go back to his post and wait for my instructions.

The hotel security manager appeared again, and I asked him to watch my post while I found out what was going on. I went into the Ops Room and found that all the radios were turned off and everyone was asleep! I found the person that was supposed to be my relief, he was rudely awoken and told in no uncertain terms to get to his post. Within minutes the rest of the sleeping beauties were awake and asking what was going on. Again, in no uncertain terms I told them exactly what was going on and then gave them a lesson on how they should conduct themselves! Making my way back to my post, two guys walked up and made a fleeting remark, which was met by a very sharp response that left them a little taken aback.

I made sure the gent was also relieved and had him taken down to the restaurant for a full breakfast, with the bill being put on the Ops Room tab. I got my own position covered, and after I briefed my relief, I proceeded to give the private security company's team leader a further lesson in the principles of close protection. I then departed, contacting the security company's office and advised them never to contact me again.

That sorry episode happened in 1998, and in 2015 a friend of mine was contacted by the same security company and was given a right royal run-around. So, seventeen years later they were still no better, but still getting the work.

# CHAPTER 10

## THE MUSIC SCENE

I was building up contacts within the security industry, and I'd become quite well known for my expertise in dealing with crowds and troublesome people. I was doing contract work for a large security company, which was mainly response teams and VIP enclosures at concerts and events.

On one job I was asked to look after the Canadian singer Bryan Adams. The concert was held at Alton Towers theme park in Staffordshire in the summer of '99. Although strictly not a close protection role, my job was to keep his compound free of any issues. I had a small team with me and we covered his inner sanctum.

I had been told that he wasn't very keen on security and we were to keep a low profile. It is always good to know what a client or principle likes or doesn't like before the job starts.

Throughout the day, which was very hot, we rotated the staff to keep them fresh and stop them getting bored. As the day progressed it got busier, and at one stage Bryan Adams came and said a quick hello. As the start of the concert drew closer and the night closed in, I changed the staff around again, putting key people in the right places - my role was to escort Bryan to and from the stage.

The head of safety from the production company popped up and said he was coming with us to the stage, which wasn't a problem with me. Bryan appeared and we moved quickly to the backstage area, where I left him with another security company who looked after backstage. I then went and stood at the front of the stage near the pit area.

The concert went off without a hitch and as he finished his set the security lads from the other company were waiting backstage for him. Well, the next thing that happened blew everyone, for he didn't go backstage, instead he ran forward and jumped into the pit area and ran around the front. And as the backstage security stood with puzzled looks on their faces, he ran right into my path. So, as he ran past I just latched on to him and ran alongside him. We ran all the way back to the compound where Lou, my 2IC was stood waiting. I'd radioed ahead and as we approached, the gate opened and Bryan ran straight into his dressing room.

The head of security came back looking quite unamused and asked me where Mr Adams was? I said tucked up safe and sound in his dressing room. He left the compound and wasn't a happy chap, but we just got on with our job.

There were a few producers knocking around at the time, and they all came up and thanked us, which was nice. Then Bryan Adams appeared and asked me where all the team were. I radioed them all in, and he personally thanked each and every one of us. He told me that we had done a great job, never got in his way, and were there when he needed us. He shook my hand, got in the car and drove off. The other security company only knew he had left when we told them, as nobody else had bothered too. There were some mixed reactions, but from our point of view it was a good job well done.

The same company tasked me to do other work for them. We did response team jobs for them at major boxing events. My job was mainly as a trouble shooter, working with the police and dealing with disorder.

Sadly, some people look at security operatives as mindless thugs, but my teams were very switched on, very proactive and extremely professional, hence why the police were always happy to have us around.

Over the years we provided not only close protection to the music industry, but also organised large scale events. These were either in fixed arenas or greenfield sites where the temporary stage and event areas were constructed. We worked on many events and pop concerts and were integral to the development of a crowd control system which not only worked, but possibly saved a lot of people from being hurt or crushed. The system was a 'safety valve' in the concert bowl or stadium concourse, basically it was a one and two-way system to stop choke points.

Over the years we covered many concerts, including:

Take That *

U2 **

Oasis

George Michael

Red Hot Chilli Peppers

Jon Bon Jovi

Rod Stewart

Celine Dion

Tom Jones

Shania Twain

Tina Turner

Diana Ross

The Eagles

The Christians ***

* During the Take That concert my wife and I were tasked to look after the well know comedian, Peter Kay. It was an interesting job to say the least as he was stood in the crowd and surrounded by thousands of people. We stood near him and lucky I had the presence of mind to put a response team nearby to create an opening if there was an issue - this was sadly overlooked at the time by the safety officer. It was a testing job, and at times a little busy shall we say, but he was happy and we managed to pull it off without any issues.

** U2 actually invited me to a talk in the USA about safety and security. However, I was working for Manchester City at the time, and the stadium safety officer asked me not to attend due to the Manchester derby taking place.

*** Prior to The Christians concert I was asked by a friend to help with security as there was a problem with the previous company. I took the job, visited the venue and built up the site plans. We put together a pit crew (another course that I wrote and gained accreditation for) and backstage security. On meeting the manager, I escorted her around the site, showing her all the areas. At the start of the concert all the staff were briefed up and in position. The band were very pleased with the levels of security presence and the event was a massive success.

Backstage with The Christians

One of my favourite outdoor concerts was for the rock band Status Quo, where I worked again with my old friend Phil Williams. I have known Phil for many years and worked with him on many events.

The concert was held in the grounds of Cyfarthfa Castle in South Wales. The set had been built and a compound constructed. My role was head of security, and to oversee safety for the event. We had over 100 staff there and our responsibilities included the pit, backstage and VIP security.

We met the band, who were housed in the castle during the warm up. They were a fantastic bunch of guys, with wicked senses of humour. We transported them to the stage in my Audi Q7.

Rick Parfitt was an avid driver and we soon got into a deep discussion about cars, in fact it went on that long that he had to be dragged on to the stage!

At the end of the show we had a five-minute slot to get the band to their coach before the police opened the roads again. My CP team including my wife Nadia, who was one of the very first females to gain the Security

Industry Association (SIA) qualification, literally ran them all the way and I think at one-point Nadia was actually carrying Francis Rossi!

We got them to the coach and on their way without anyone knowing what had gone on, and to top off a brilliant event, Nadia got a big thank you and smacking kiss from Francis Rossi.

# CHAPTER 11

## TV and FILM

The most popular bodyguards are the ones you see with the pop stars. Normally they are of large build, and are there to make sure their client doesn't get approached by autograph hunters.

Part of the job is making sure the VIP gets from one place to another, sometimes without leaving the building. This was the case at a film premier we were involved in at a large shopping mall. The premier was very busy, with a lot of busy areas that were difficult to control. The route was mapped out by red carpet which in itself was a problem, not for us, but the event security.

Our job was to escort the cast into the venue, make sure that they weren't harassed and keep them moving. That can be a difficult situation because VIPs need to interact with the public otherwise they don't stay in good stead with their fans. So, it requires the right balance between keeping them moving and giving them the time they need to engage with the fans. On this occasion the role itself was not that difficult, and the VIPs were very accommodating and worked with our team.

A big crowd had gathered, mainly autograph hunters and normal fans. I assigned my wife Nadia to look after one of the main singers from the pop group Blue. Watching the crowd, Nadia realised that there was a lot of young girls, which was not unusual, but one in particular was paying close attention to the large ring on the singer's finger. The girl then moved forward and grabbed the hand with the ring on. Nadia very quickly moved in, covered his hand and moved it out of harm's way. The gent had no idea what was going but he was lucky that Nadia was on the ball.

In 1998, I was involved with the very first film premier in Manchester, and it was on that job that I met a guy from London called Jerry Judge. Jerry became a good work contact and a person I also trained for his SIA qualification. Jerry's company Music & Arts Security Ltd, provides security for all the big red-carpet events and if anyone needs looking after, he does it.

On this event I was helping out a contact who wanted a person who knew the ropes. As the job unfolded the London team did their job and I just did what I normally do. It was getting late and I was asked by Jerry if I could help him out, as he had to go to the next venue in Birmingham and asked if I would take over the event, which was a surprise. I agreed and there it started and the job went well.

The picture opposite is of Jerry Judge carrying out a vehicle search on one of my courses. He also brought up a number of students with him, many who to this day look after the likes of Johnny Depp and Gary Barlow.

I was contacted by the TV talent show, X-Factor, to provide protection for one of the finalists while he was in Manchester. At the time we were their preferred security supplier and had already done the audition shows with them. The X-Factor's producers were always very happy with how we looked after them.

The person we were asked to look after was Shayne Ward. He was a Manchester lad and would go on to win the competition. There were a number of venues that had to be visited. The first thing we did was establish points of contact at the venues and get an understanding of the event.

The people at the main venue were very accommodating, and pleased that we had went in advance to introduce ourselves, rather than just turning up on the day. We carried out a walk of the venue, the stage area and all the debus points. We also looked at areas to secure the client if needed.

Shayne arrived by helicopter on the morning of the event. The day started with a trip to the school that he had gone to. It was very low key, but very emotional, not only for him but also the staff and the children. Apart from when the children rushed forward to meet him, there was no threat to him, so it was just a case of letting them all enjoy themselves.

During the day Shayne wanted to go to a shop while the others were having lunch. It was an off the beat request, but we did it anyway. There were no issues and people were just wishing him well. As we went to cross the road in Peter Street some builders shouted at him, he turned to look at them and didn't see a car coming. I actually had to grab him and pull him back – luckily all was well, but it was a reminder of how easily it is for them to get distracted.

We then visited his local area where there was a large gathering of well-wishers, in situations like this everyone is happy but you have to keep in mind any jealousy from others. Being on your toes will deter people, but you have to be aware of your surroundings at all times.

When we arrived at the main venue the stewards and security had formed a barrier, and there were no issues.

The event was a massive success and Shayne performed his winning song. After leaving the venue Shayne kindly offered to drop me off at home, much to the shock of my wife and her friends as they watched Shayne rocking up outside our house. We gave him a bottle of champagne and wished him well. Many years later I was having lunch in the Trafford Centre and Shayne was sat opposite me with his partner. As I was leaving I asked him how he was doing. He looked at me and said he was good thanks, and then he recognised me. He gave me a great big hug, shook my hand and explained that he that was just telling his partner about the event all those years before, how spooky was that!

After the event, Sarah Anderson, the X-Factor production co-ordinator for Thames Television, provided the following reference:

Phil Moulton with his company Exclusafe provided us with a friendly and efficient service and we would be more than happy to use them again for any future events where the security of our production team, crew and the public is paramount.

# CHAPTER 12

## MARTIN MCGUINNESS

Not all jobs that I was involved in were star studded. This job was a particularly sensitive one. In 2001, I was asked by one of the UK's largest security and event organisers to look after Martin McGuinness, the former IRA member turned politician, who at that time was Minister of Education in the Northern Ireland Executive.

My job was to ensure there were no issues while he attended an event in Warrington. The event was a Christmas Carol Concert, after which he would be meeting the parents of Tim Parry and Johnathon Ball, two young lads who had been killed when the IRA set off two bombs in the centre of Warrington in 1993.

The security company said that the job was out of their comfort zone, which in fairness I understood, as it took me a while to get two lads to work with me on it.

Although it was only a short job, it was very intense and involved a great deal of planning, all of which went on behind closed doors. I did an advance recce on the venue and met with the head of security. We put plans in place for safe rooms and routes. Although there was no intelligence to suggest there might be a threat, we had to plan for the worst-case scenario.

Our role was to shadow him, but without being overbearing. As Martin McGuinness arrived a large crowd, including some protestors, had gathered. We cleared the route and ensured it was a quick walk through. He was accompanied by two other people and although there was an element of calm, it was a very surreal feeling.

We were placed around the venue to watch the crowd and to remove him if there was a problem. I think it was unnerving for many who were there, so it stayed quiet apart from the singing.

We escorted him around for the brief time he was there, I remembered he met a TV presenter in a room with the parents. Our job was to secure it, and make sure they weren't interrupted.

After a very short time he emerged and headed for the exit. We secured the route again and my role was to escort him to the car. He didn't make any comments, but the weird thing was that once he was in the car it stopped about ten feet away from me, the window wound down and Martin McGuiness popped his head out and said cheers to the lads, waved and drove off. He is probably only one of a few who have actually thanked me.

# CHAPTER 13

## EXCLUSAFE

I started my own company with two aims, firstly - offering close protection services to clients; and secondly - developing and delivering close protection and personal safety training courses.

Getting started wasn't easy. I still had some problems from the marriage that I had walked away from. I left with nothing apart from three bin liners that contained my worldly possessions. I was living in rented accommodation, and had just left a job that had been frustrating me. So, when I first set up the company I started with nothing, not even an overdraft.

As the company grew I worked hard to gain more contracts, which included me providing night time security at the five-star Lowry Hotel. After I finished my shift, I would then teach people either close protection or personal safety. I did this to help others attain a qualification that would normally be out of their reach due to the costs and the fact that not many people were running the courses. I got a lot of satisfaction out of doing that, especially as I knew from my own experience that such courses were expensive and at that time you could only get them through the company that promised you work if you attended one of theirs.

As my portfolio increased I started to focus on designing training courses. I wrote an outline for a close protection course which I wanted to gain national accreditation for. At the time there were no recognised close protection qualifications apart from those obtained by the military or police. With this in mind, I approached the Manchester College of Arts and Technology (MANCAT).

They had already been approached by a contact of mine, but they had dismissed his proposal as it wasn't what they were looking for. When I put my case together it was based on the planning of an operation, the law, understanding the threat etc. It took some time to convince them to listen to what I was proposing, but eventually I had a meeting with them.

I put together my proposal and attended a meeting at the offices of the Greater Manchester Open College Network (GMOCN), where we discussed the finer points. Finally, I went in front of a panel from the police, law and academics who interviewed me for over four hours – grilling me on the content, my background and the aims of the course.

I was very proud when they accepted my proposal and my course was granted a Level 2, the equivalent to an NVQ Level 2. The course was then rolled out and it was used from 2001 to 2005, until the SIA course superseded it.

We held courses nearly every month with up to ten students on each one. We ran them from a house in north Manchester called Malcolm House, which had room for twelve students. The courses ran as if it was an actual operation, with the students sometimes working through the night. They were taught how to set up an operation, secure venues, carry out recces, and a whole lot more. They also had to complete a large workbook which I still use today.

We had people travel from all over the UK to attend the training and it was great. To see the students' progress, and gain qualifications which would enable them to have a career in close protection, was very rewarding.

One of my favourite students was my wife Nadia. She completed the course and went on to help me run our company. Nadia successfully completed a number of tasks including witness protection and looking after a family who had been seriously threated. She also looked after Victoria Beckham, Donny Osmond, Blue, Status Quo, Peter Kay and a number of other nice little jobs – I am very proud of her.

When the SIA came into force I wanted to push the close protection courses more than anything. I had spoken to the awarding body about my courses and then wrote another updated version for the SIA.

At my offices in Urmston in Manchester we had a visit from a lady from the SIA. She had come to inspect the course, myself, and the training. She was really impressed by the whole set up and looked through the content of the course I had written. She also asked about my seven year's teaching experience and looked at the course that I had already done through MANCAT.

The course was then sent to the awarding body EDXCEL BTEC. In the meantime, I had arranged to run a course in the United States. Nadia and I paid for two students to come with us. We planned to use it as a bit of an exercise, and with some of my contacts over there we planned firearms courses. As we arrived in the US we got notification that my SIA course had been granted accreditation as a BTEC Level 3 course. I was very pleased and proud of what we had achieved.

We stayed in the US for a week and I was very pleased with the way the course had gone. In addition, we carried out recces and Nadia worked hard on her own drills. When it came to the firearms training, the students that we brought with us didn't have any money so Nadia paid for them on her credit cards, and I paid for mostly everything else.

My courses cover many aspects of close protection, the most important factor here is that I use real life scenarios and experiences when delivering the lessons.

There are many training companies who still offer the 'ghost course' - where the student rocks up money in hand and the exams are more or less done for them.

My courses have attracted students from a variety of backgrounds including the armed forces, special forces, the police, VIP security experts and many more. Over the years I have trained over 2500 students, and helped others who couldn't afford to pay the outrageous prices some companies were charging.

Nadia on a firearms course in the United States

The company name started to become well thought of, and the Manchester City Council started using me to teach personal safety and awareness. They also asked me to provide witness protection for people who were being intimidated.

Although the company was only small, we started to pick up more and more work including our first big contract, which was with Stockport County Football Club. We also provided a troubleshooting team for world championship boxing events held at the Manchester Velodrome and the MEN Arena.

Around this time, I was approached by some of Nadia's clients (she was working for Selfridges) who were interested in what I was doing. Two of which were a former police superintendent and an army major. After some discussions they asked me to join forces with them, which I did.

Shortly after this we picked up contracts for Manchester City FC and Leeds United FC. We provided two response teams of sixteen staff, for both clubs for each home game – as a company we were getting bigger every week.

It was at that time that I went to the 2002 World Karate Championships in Las Vegas. When I arrived in the States, I received a text message from one of the partners saying he was having personal problems and had decided to leave the company. I was devastated, but did what I had to do and finished fourth in the world.

It was at this point that I set up Exclusafe Ltd on my own. I arranged with the bank for a small overdraft of £5000. The business grew and we gained more contracts. We then become accredited to train our own staff, as well as other peoples. We furnished the offices into classrooms for teaching and training, again this came from our own money and the problem with available cashflow was never far away. The main problem was that we had 100 staff that were being mainly used for our football club contracts. All the staff needed uniforms and some specialist equipment.

Again, this was paid for from our own money and credit cards.

Despite the financial challenges, we had built up a large company – mainly on the back of my experience and knowledge. We'd developed training courses that were being used worldwide and my dream was coming true.

# CHAPTER 14

## CLOSE PROTECTION

I was working with an agent who was trying to get into CP work. He asked me to do some work for a local social service in Manchester – details of which I can't disclose. The issue was with a lady who had a problem with a female member of staff. The matter was concerning the custody of her child.

The lady, who was from Somalia, was short in height but quite a robust person. For a few weeks I had been at the Centre, supporting the team. Then one day I got a call asking me to be there early as they were expecting trouble from her.

After getting to the centre I stood behind the bullet proof glass as she walked into the waiting room and threw a large lump of rock at the glass. There were two people sat in the waiting room and it was like a sketch from a comedy show - they just sat there and didn't move. I ran out and pulled them into the office and the lady ran out, shutting the door behind her.

I thought that was it, but oh no! Outside she produced a machete and starting carving into cars and trees outside the office. I don't know what possessed me but I opened the door and chased her up the street until she stopped and smacked the blade into a tree. The police arrived shortly after and she was arrested and bailed. However, that wasn't the end of her, she carried out a number of other attacks, the last of which was when she firebombed the office!

My role in the anti-social behaviour order (ASBO) teams became quite prominent and I put together a number of packages for supplying trained security staff. The job of the staff was to protect witnesses who were being intimidated by gangs or others. This often involved threats to life, guns and drugs so we had to be on the top of our game.

There were many occasions when I was away on family holidays only to get a call to arrange security cover. All the staff had gone through my CP course and other forms of training, we risk assessed everything and put in place safe areas and patrols. I devised a training programme called Breakaway-Moves, which I had rolled out over the years under a different name. I was asked to deliver this programme as a pilot scheme to a group of wardens, which I did. At the time I didn't know that I was being watched by the Head of Training at Manchester Housing. After the course she told me that she delivered a nationally recognised programme which was similar to mine, but she said that my course contained a lot more in the area of breaking away. I ended up running this course for all of Manchester ASBO teams, neighbourhood wardens, social services, and then a few years later to members of football clubs.

This lasted for over eleven years, with my company becoming a preferred supplier for many government agencies dealing with ASBOs. This also included surveillance where we would monitor behaviour and write up statements for court orders. We were that well respected the Crown Prosecution Service gave us a great deal of credit for cracking a number of issues.

When taking on a protection detail it is important to ask the client if they have been, or had a feeling that they were being followed, and if they'd received any threats. If this is the case you need to assume that somebody has your client's details, therefore the home or office is at threat, and possibly the people in or around those places.

We carried out a witness protection operation on a South Manchester estate, where the client had received a number of death threats. Concerningly the threats had been made to her face. In this case the threat is viable and could be carried out by the perpetrator. Because of her location a resident security team (RST) was put in place and support given to her when she attended court. We were aware of the perpetrator following her and waiting for an opportunity to make an attack. In this case we assigned a CPO and an RST to be with her throughout her ordeal. When she attended court, we used a local taxi company to pick us up at the very last minute. This was done to disrupt any type of surveillance by the perpetrator. The more random we can make things, the more chance we have of flushing them out.

On another job, this time on a North Manchester estate, the witnesses were a group who had made a complaint against a known gangster who dealt in stolen goods. This problem arose because they lived next door to the perpetrator. On arrival to carry out the risk assessment I was met by a small number of workmen sheeting up the flat, my first question was have the witnesses gone? To my astonishment the answer was no, and that they were still inside. They had received a threat that they were going to get burnt out, and because all the windows had been put in, the workmen were boarding them up with plywood sheets!

Without waiting I made two calls, one to my team who were on the way over, the second to the client advising them of the dangerous situation. Within five minutes of arriving, a group of youths on bikes had gathered outside with what can only be described as petrol bombs. When my team arrived the two cars were quickly brought to the house door and the witnesses hastily put in the back - two males in one and two females in the other. I used my own car a rolling block, and we got away literally minutes before the flat was attacked.

There was one family in particular that we carried out security for over a long period of time. Due to the sensitivity of the issue I won't disclose the name, but will refer to the lady involved as DH. The remit of the job was two-fold. Primary was close protection of DH and her three children. Her husband had gone missing one day while on his way to work. His car was never found and neither was he. The secondary part was to investigate his disappearance, which also included trying to locate a very large boat in the South of France.

After an initial phone call a meeting with DH was arranged. She was so scared of being followed that we met in a large shopping centre. Due to the seriousness of the situation we contacted the police who had been dealing with the case. I arranged a meeting, and they explained that they had got nowhere with it. In fact, it had gotten so bad for DH that she had even put up a £250,000 reward to try and find her husband.

The job lasted for six months and over that time I had put in place a resident security team who lived in a static caravan on site. Everywhere DH went, I was with her. The children were watched constantly, and we had trackers on her phones.

We spent a lot of time researching the situation and trying to locate the missing boat, which was worth about £1.5 million. However, we weren't having much luck and then one day we had a meeting with the senior police officer in charge of the case. He basically warned me off the job, informing me that DH's father was connected to a Middle East terrorist group. However, we did carry on and things slowly started to unfold. We interviewed a number of people, passed the information onto the police but still couldn't get to the bottom of things.

One of our guards strangely enough was attacked in his own home, and suffered a number of injures, this was thought to be unrelated to the job, but was worrying at the time. The guards on the RST were rotated around, and were briefed up about taking precautions themselves.

The family were transported around using a combination of an MPV and 4 x 4, but they never travelled together in the same car. At one stage DH went overseas to meet her father in the Middle East. So as not to cause issues, spotters were put on her from a different location. The job also took us to Paris where another meeting was arranged with her father, who we were never disclosed to. When we arrived in Paris we had two spotters sat in a café, their brief was to monitor us and see if we were being followed – which we were!

The meeting never took place as DH's father never showed up. Myself and two females followed DH through the streets of Paris while our spotter hung back and watched our backs.

The trip went off without any issues and when DH got back to the UK she posed a number of questions to her father, some of which were quite shocking. At that point we increased her security. Every movement was covered and when she went in our car we had no visible back up, as it followed on from a different point.

The job stretched into Christmas and we spent most of our time with DH and her family. In fact, it got to a point when DH asked my wife that if anything happened to her, would she take her children and look after them! This was a complete shock as we tried to keep it strictly business and not personal. Thankfully it never came to that and eventually DH left the country. We believe she fled in fear for her own safety, she did however, contact the police to say she was ok, but also left with a large amount of her father's funds.

# CHAPTER 15

# THE FOOTBALL ASSOCIATION

In 2004 I became one of two security providers to the Football Association, providing security for the England Senior and U21 teams.

This came about when I was asked by Manchester City Football Club to provide security at their training ground. This was in preparation for a mini tournament being played between England, Iceland and Japan in Manchester. The tournament, which took place between the 30th of May and 5th of June was played at The City of Manchester Stadium, and was part of England's preparation for the 2004 European

Championships being held in Portugal later in the month.

Our task was to stop the media from taking photographs of the England team while they were training. I had carried out the initial recce and identified some weak areas. I proposed to put teams of our staff in the woods surrounding the training ground. The plan was for their presence to act as a deterrent to the members of the press who might try to use the woods to their advantage.

The proposal was accepted, and the job went well without any issues, and the FA were really pleased with how we had performed. Over time we covered a number of events for them including kit launches, personal appearances, player's weddings and the build up to Euro 2004. The FA's head of security, Ray Whitworth, commented that I was one of only two providers in the UK trusted with this, so that was a real boost for me and the company.

During the lead up to the Euro's we were deployed at the team's hotel, which was the Lowry in Manchester, and the role of my twelve-man team was quite specific: meet and greet; act as a buffer for the press; liaise with the managers and team members; and ensure that there were no security breaches in the area.

During that time, we had a very special visit from His Royal Highness Prince William. The security team secured all the floors, and the normal protocols were put in place. Our role was to support certain security teams and agencies that were present there.

This part of my life and the picture above holds many memories. My mum had phoned me a few hours before Prince William's arrival and told me my stepbrother Jimmy had suffered bleeding on the brain, and had only a short time to live. I had to stay on the post because of the prince's arrival and remained there until the visit was complete and the area cleared. I went to the hospital, where I sat with Jimmy, shared a few moments with him and promised that I would be back to see him again.

Prior to the team departing for the Euro's we were given the job to look after the team's kit – hardly the most exciting of jobs you'd think. We were given instructions to go to a certain room in the Lowry, where on arrival we found it to be empty apart from a table. We were told to secure the empty room, so after doing a complete sweep and search for anything that shouldn't be there, I placed one person inside and another one outside.

The plan was that the kit van would turn up late at night, but what we didn't know was that it would be followed by a coach carrying the England players. When the kit van and the players turned up the lads made a hasty call to me, and then quickly secured the venue. I was walking into the hotel at the time, but we acted quickly and soon found out that our duties had escalated from looking after the kit to ensuring the team was not compromised.

We kept the area clear, but the biggest challenge was securing the players because the room we were using at the time, was actually the departure lounge for the flight to Portugal, and once they were through the customs area that had been set up they had to be kept sterile. It was a good test which I believe we passed with flying colours, because for the next nine years I ran a team of security staff for the FA through my company.

While the England team were in Portugal I was given a task that was short on detail to say the least. All I knew was a Manchester United player had suffered an injury and was returning for treatment.

At the time I was on a family holiday in the Lake District. I was picked up by my driver and headed back to Manchester to start the job. I received a briefing that detailed the task. We were to provide security teams to leap frog each venue, securing the areas and routes, prior to the player's arrival. Security was tight and I wasn't given the details by the FA until the very last minute, as the whole thing was to be kept quiet.

My team met me with no idea where we were going, but on arrival at the hospital the staff were aware of us, and said that they had already had a visit from a 'security team'. The player's visit had been leaked by someone and it was front page news in the papers: 'The FA employs foot soldiers to guard Rooney' was the headlines. We had no idea who had leaked it, although we did have our suspicions but couldn't prove it.

The job had been challenging because our contact didn't share the locations until the very last minute, but we performed our roles fantastically and without any issues, and we were thanked by Wayne Rooney himself.

After it was over I went back to the Lake District to continue my holiday. I returned home a few days later with a promise to go and see Jimmy. Sadly, I got a call from his partner saying that he had slipped away quietly. He was a Manchester United fan and we later spread his ashes on the pitch at Old Trafford.

During the tour Euro's I did get a phone call from Ray Whitworth from the FA, and was asked I if would be the main security provider for them. As you can imagine I grabbed the opportunity with both hands, and this was the start of some great adventures, trips overseas and working with some fantastic people. Which even included being presented with a token of thanks from the Guardia Civil police while working with them in Spain.

I was also tasked a number of times to look after David Beckham. One time when he came back from Spain I picked him up during the night at the private airfield at Manchester Airport. There were also a number of times when he was being harassed and followed, that I was asked to meet the head of security at the hotel where he was staying to ensure he got there safely.

We arranged to meet him and secured a discrete entrance, however we encountered a problem when an unauthorised person latched on to the party. The person, who had another arrangement with David Beckham, but one that was not recognised by the FA, was stopped at the barrier, where we secured him. I spoke to him and advised him the FA did not want his involvement, but I did the professional thing and thanked him and sent him on his way.

# CHAPTER 16

# FOOTBALL CLUBS

Over the years we were the preferred security suppliers for a number of football clubs including:

Manchester City FC

Bolton Wanderers FC

Leeds United FC

Blackburn Rovers FC

Our roles ranged from the tunnel security, response teams, access control, and we even covered plain clothes security in the crowd. I designed a surveillance course for dealing with anti-social behaviour among the spectators. We supplied staff who were dressed in plain clothes to deal with this, they were all well trained and knew about the law and taking statements. We were very successful in our operations, some of which resulted in banning orders.

Over the years I also worked with Manchester United Football Club. Those contracts weren't close protection jobs but very high-profile corporate events. I worked alongside the stadium safety officer (SSO) at the club, where we created a sterile area for large Christmas events catering up to 1500 people. The planning was carried out by myself and we worked together with the events team for five years. I am really proud to say we had only one incident, which was handbags and nothing more. Arthur Roberts, the SSO at the club wrote me a fantastic reference congratulating me and my company for our professional services.

# CHAPTER 17

## MANCHESTER CITY FOOTBALL CLUB

During the nine years that I was involved with Manchester City I was entrusted with many jobs and events involving the players and the team. This came about when Clare Marsden, the player liaison officer at the club, asked if I could help out with an event.

The players were having a Christmas party at the Radisson hotel in Manchester. I used to look after the security for that hotel and the job involved keeping the areas clear and ensuring that there was no interference from the public. I agreed, and met with the hotel manager and event organiser, who both knew and trusted me.

The event was quite a lavish affair so we tied down the whole area. Using my knowledge of the hotel I positioned my staff in areas that were best for observation and control. As the guests arrived there was a great deal of interest around the team, but we had it boxed off so to speak, and there were no issues or interference, and the event went like a dream.

Shortly after the event the liaison officer contacted me again and asked if I could provide some staff to look after the football team who were going to Tenerife. As I was busy running the company I had to delegate a number of trusted staff to go with them.

I spoke with the stadium safety officer, who at the time wasn't happy, but since it was the manager of the football team who had requested that my company did the job, he had to agree to it.

I carried out the risk assessments, put together all the feasibility studies, contacted all the people I needed to and devised a set of protocols for my team with regards to security, standing operating procedures (SOPs), health and safety, and communications. The trip lasted for a number of days and my staff were in constant comms with me throughout which I in turn relayed to the club, from which there was some fantastic feedback.

The job was a great success and it was a role that we carried out throughout the following seasons. Clare Marsden was really supportive throughout, every time the team travelled we were responsible for their security.

Each trip was risk assessed and a full feasibility study carried out, which was then hand delivered to the training ground prior to them leaving. I organised the security at the train stations through Virgin Trains who were really supportive and helpful.

The club ambassador was also given a full brief, and we travelled to many hotels and football grounds. I also organised the collection of the team and transport to get them home from the private aircraft. This included on many occasions the football manager, head of communications and team members.

Throughout the season we were given fantastic reviews by the manager and players, who came to really trust and have confidence in me and my services.

The contract with Manchester City turned out to be one of my biggest ones, with sometimes around one hundred staff on each match. Our very first game was the last Manchester derby played at Maine Road. During that match we had a small team of twelve whose job was to act as trouble spotters in the stadium.

We very quickly grew in numbers and the close protection courses I ran served as a fantastic recruitment system. All our staff had five days CP training, on which I covered things such as the law, conflict management and protection duties. The company started getting more and more recognised, and because of the professionalism we demonstrated, we picked up contract after contract.

After Manchester City moved to their new stadium our numbers then grew to fifty staff at each match. I was asked by the SSO at the time to draw up plans and operation details which I did. We then took over more contracts at the club providing customer service staff as well as security staff for the tunnel, response teams, access control and many other areas.

We were also asked to look after the player's homes by personal invitation, but we encountered a barrier here as the SSO began to feel as though he was being left out of the loop, but that was not the case, as he was informed from day one (more about this later).

In June 2007, Thaksin Shinawatra, the former Prime Minister of Thailand, bought Manchester City Football Club. On one occasion we were tasked to look after him by the head of operations and the SSO.

The job was quite extensive. Firstly, we had to pick him up after he landed at the ground in his private helicopter. Then we took him to a number of locations, where we had carried recces and advanced work, all of which was quite straight forward.

We were then tasked to provide security for him at a concert in honour of him taking over the club, the SSO asked me to arrange a couple of recces around the event site which was in Manchester city centre. These sites were elevated above the venue stage area and gave us a bird's eye view.

Then he arranged for me to visit Manchester Town Hall and Heron House. My job was to scope the area, fix positions, risk assess the points and look at sweepers in the area of the elevated posts - which were linked to response teams in the crowd via radio.

On the day of the event our job was to watch the area for potential issues or trouble in the crowd. I briefed the team and issued them the following kit:

Safety harness and support
Mobile phones and radios
Binoculars
Note pads
Waterproofs
Welfare kit

I was then asked to attend the control room, where I was greeted by two police officers who did not look at all happy, the club's SSO was also sat there. When I asked what the problem was the senior officer asked me if I had staff in Manchester at the moment. I said I did and he asked what equipment do they have. Feeling slightly uneasy I said, 'Radios, phones, safety harnesses, binoculars and waterproofs, why?'

The officers asked if they had anything else, and I said no, and again asked them why they wanted to know that. Again, they said nothing. So, then I dropped the bombshell and told them that the operation had been set up by the SSO days before. And just to prove it, I went to where I kept my briefing sheets and showed them the hard copies, to which they both replied 'Fantastic Phil'. It turned out that they had not been told about the event and that's why they weren't happy!

The next thing was even funnier - Thaksin Shinawatra had a guy who was brought in by the owners of a Thai restaurant. The guy was a Thai boxer, very strong and looked the part, but when the police officers asked what his drills were if there was an issue, he calmly replied 'I will knock them out of the way!'

151

As we got to the venue the SSO was in the car with us. The event was being run by an event security company that I had known for many years, ran by a guy that I knew and had encountered many times - I would say he was a friend more than a contact. But when we arrived we soon found that there were no arrangements in place to get Mr Shinawatra to and from the stage. This hadn't been planned and was not part of my brief. Again, the Thai boxer turned around and offered an option which was instantly dismissed. He was then advised that his opinions weren't wanted and to leave it to myself and the others. The moral of the story here is always use the right people for the right job.

In September 2008 Mr Shinawatra sold Manchester City to the Abu Dhabi United Group. During a visit to the stadium by the new owners I came across a Special Branch officer called Shep, who I knew from a previous job I'd done with him.

Shep was now working for the club and was in charge of security for the owners - I'd previously been told by the SSO that the new owners had their own protection team in place and that I was to keep out of the way and not to get involved.

As the owners approached I noticed Shep. I nodded to him, which he replied in kind, and he and the party went into the VIP lift, which my eldest son Callam was looking after. At the time I was stood with a gentleman, who was my number two, and a short while later Shep came back down the lift. We greeted each other and exchanged professional comments. I introduced him to Callam, explained that he was my son, and told him that he would help him in any way he could. Shep then turned to Callam and kindly said 'you're learning from the master', as he pointed to me. Well, my number two's jaw dropped and he was speechless.

# CHAPTER 18

## PLAYER PROTECTION

Close protection means more than just guarding a person. On many occasions I have organised last minute trips, secured venues and dealt with existing security at nightclubs, bars and restaurants - mostly on my own, or with a driver if lucky. One football player even gave me the keys to his safe, which although was very thoughtful, was a worrying time for me.

I have protected and supported a lot of football players, and many have trusted me to look after their family members as well. Gretar Steinsson, the Bolton Wanderers player, whose wife was Miss Iceland, asked me to make sure she was picked up from the airport.

On arrival I got a text message from his wife saying she was poorly on the aircraft. I contacted Gretar and asked if there were any other issues that had happened, or anything we should be aware of. I then spoke with the airport who said that they couldn't do anything until the aircraft had landed. At that point I got another text saying the aircrew were giving her medical attention. We then arranged for an ambulance to be on site when the aircraft landed.

We were there to meet her when she arrived and had her swiftly transported to a local hospital. We stayed with her until she was well enough to be released and then transported her home. Gretar didn't know how to repay us - but that was just what we did.

In late 2000s there were a spate of attacks on football players houses and families. One of which was on the home of Manchester City's Micah Richards. His house had been broken into, but strangely the only thing that was stolen was a set of keys. Fortunately, there was no one in the house at the time, but after that, Micah's family looked to me for support and advice, not only on security but also how to look after themselves.

Micah's cousin, Armani, who was a close friend of my son, wanted to become an accountant. At the time we had our own accounts team, and we took Armani on as a junior. The funniest thing was when he came to my office, I went to get him a drink and returned to see him stood open mouthed looking at all my pictures, references and certificates. He stood there and said 'I thought you were just a manager you really do all the bodyguarding don't you!'

Micah wrote the following testimony:

We have been using Phil and his company Exclusafe for nearly a year now. The main purpose for me using them is that in my eyes they can make me feel as safe and secured as much as possible in and around my own home. But not just that, the service and how professional they are as a company, is second to none as far as I have seen. All their staff have a likeable factor and are very highly trained, which I believe you need as most of the security they do for me is in and around my home. Where family members who live with me all share the same view. I seem to have built up a great relationship with Phil and his company as they often do security for both Manchester City and England U21 games. So now it's almost like whenever there is a problem, or I need security, I can rely on Exclusafe to provide me with some of the most honest and trustworthy security guards at the drop of a hat. I would definitely advise anyone who needs any form of security service in and around their home to use Exclusafe.

Yours faithfully,
Micah Richards.


On another occasion, while my wife Nadia and I were out at a hotel, I got a call from Manchester City's SSO who asked me to get some security over to a player's home. The wife of the Manchester City player, Roque Santa Cruz, had suffered a nasty attack and a number of men had broken into the family home with the children present. The so-called tough guys had held his wife at knifepoint in front of her children. I deployed two staff straight away to secure the house, and the police were soon on the scene which made the family more at ease. I made my way over to meet the family in what was to be the start of a three-year job protecting them. I looked after the family, their home, arranged security for events, nights out and fashion show visits for his wife. We were trusted to the point that Nadia, who was also a Close Protection Officer at the time, looked after his wife while she was pregnant. Roque Santa Cruz wrote the following testimony:

To whom it may concern Phil Moulton and his company Exclusafe have provided for my family and me security for the past two years. I have found the service reliable and trustworthy, if you require any further information please do not hesitate to contact me.

There was another time when I got another call from the SSO. He had received intelligence that there was going to be another attack at Roque's house that night. I got straight on to it and put four staff outside his house.

It was a winter evening and I was in my car, parked on the driveway. From my position I could see homes that were owned by other players. They were not my clients anymore as my contract had been snatched by a person whose actions I would really have enjoyed sharing, I didn't because that could have put people at risk - but that's another story.

As I sat there in my Audi Q7, which gave me a great command position, I noticed a car slipping into the road. It came down the Hale Stanhope Road, and then its lights went off. I watched closely as it slowly approached the house of a player that I had previously guarded. I watched as it stopped and my actions then were to force their hand. I started my car and drove past the parked car, as I passed I saw two males dressed all in black sat in the front. I kept going and then turned the car around, and slowly drove up behind them with all my lights on. But just as I did that another car T-barred them and two burly guys got out and quickly removed the two men from the car. The burly men were undercover police officers and they recognised me straight away. 'We'll sort it Phil,' they said.

I found out later that the two men were from a security company that was employed by the person who had taken my contract. How do I know? Because they told me!

I sat watching the police deal with them - smiling I suppose. When the police finished with them they drove up and parked opposite me. I got out and challenged them both, and asked what they were doing. 'We were told to watch Roque's house,' they said. I explained professionally that he was my client and pointed out that they had in fact been watching the wrong house on the wrong side of the road! When I asked them who had told them to watch Roque's house they handed me a piece of lined paper with names and addresses on it, which they said had been given to them by the club's SSO. Needless to say, I dismissed them quickly, but the incident confirmed that the SSO had it in for me and my company.

As I mentioned earlier the SSO seemed to have a problem with me looking after the player's houses and this issue began the demise of my contract at the club, as we were eventually replaced by another company. I was later informed by the directors of that company that the SSO had told them that they were doing the team security as it was his call. I wished them good luck and was very proud of the time that we'd spent looking after the players.

I really enjoyed all the years that I worked for Manchester City Football Club and hopefully one day I can rekindle my working relationship with them.

# CHAPTER 19

## LEEDS UNITED FOOTBALL CLUB

One day I got a call from the managing director of a security company asking if I had a team available for a specific job that night - this was at 2.30 in the afternoon. Although it was short notice, I said I could, and called a few of my team. Not long after we travelled to Leeds, where the football manager of Leeds United Football Club, was having some issues with some of the Leeds supporters - now there is a surprise!

Our job was to monitor the crowd at the match that evening. Myself and two others sat behind the dugout and created a presence, we had the few fans who did a bit of shouting, but us being there helped calm the situation. The job went very well, and the manager was really happy.

The funny thing about this was that the company who asked me, were actually doing that job, but we managed it without any problems and they obviously couldn't. I then got a call to do another job for them at a match on the following Saturday. Again, it was short notice, but I got a team of eight together, this time on arriving at the ground we were told that we were being used as car park staff. No disrespect to car park attendants, but I said 'No, we're not doing that, so we'll be off back to Manchester!'

The next moment a lady came up with an earpiece in, and asked me what the problem was. I asked who she was and she told me she was the assistant safety officer.

I told her it was my understanding that we were there to do the same job as we did the other evening. She replied telling me that we would be put where we were needed.

I told her we didn't work for the security company and that we are normally drafted in to deal with problems. She was unaware of this, and not happy, so we carried on walking away. She called me back and in a more appreciative manner asked if we could deal with a problem area for her. Which of course we did, and again got a great report.

I got another call to attend the stadium later that week and was told not to discuss it with anyone. On arrival I was asked to wait in a very important looking office where I then met the stadium safety officer. We had a very candid chat about security, and then he told me that he wanted to try me out to see how good we were. The test was the tunnel area, dressing rooms and the manager's security. I then asked him about the other security company. He replied that they were not the best and that they needed to be changed.

I took the job. Firstly, we secured the tunnel area and then introduced SOPs that were not in place. The former head of security would not share information or protocols leaving me with no option but to come down hard and revamp everything. We increased our role to protecting the manager when he was under threat, and my good mate Pete Dwan, protected the chairman, Peter Ridsdale's home and family.

One day we were urgently called to the chairman's house due to some nasty threats from fans. We arrived very quickly in Pete's MPV, which was all black and shiny. The chairman met us at the entry and we had a look around the house and grounds. We agreed it would be best if we situated ourselves outside the house. We then spoke to the chairman's wife, she was a really nice lady who asked if have we done this sort of thing before? To which Pete answered 'No luv we do this off the cuff!' I am sorry, but those words will stay with me forever!

The police turned up in a Land Rover, and being a little mischievous we sat back and watched a young PC do his patrol. We then got out of the car, and the poor lad just stood there. We explained who we were and I think I heard a sigh of relief. The job on the chairman's house went on for about another two weeks – football, what a wonderful sport!

We ended up spending six years at the football club, we carried out undercover work, arranged event security for the players and their families, and it ended up being a nice job.

# CHAPTER 20

# A ROYAL VISIT

In March 2008 I was given three hours' notice to put a security team together, for a visit to the Manchester Velodrome by His Royal Highness Prince Edward. In that time, I located a safe room for the principle, identified an IAD route in case of an emergency, and arranged swift exit points.

I was very honoured to be able to assist the party, and once the advance team arrived, I briefed them on my proposed measures. They were more than pleased, and agreed every action that I'd put in place.

On the door, I put two of my security staff who vetted people on the way in, while I checked the perimeters and maintained my position near to the Special Branch team. Fortunately, I knew the location well and this helped the whole operation.

This was my first time working alongside Special Branch. Although it was a privilege, my main focus was ensuring the event ran well. We cleared all the areas, carried out physical sweeps and then secured them – informing the others of what we had done at all times.

On Prince Edward's arrival I stood in the background, covering the front entrance with my other two staff in the enclosure. The visit went off without a hitch and our performance at what was very short notice was recognised by the velodrome's General Manager in his very kind words below:

I have worked with Phil Moulton for several years in various capacities and can highly recommend his services. Whilst I was Operations Manager of the Sportcity site, I regularly used Phil and his company for the supply of security staff during major events. I have also used the company for events in my current position as General Manager of the Manchester Velodrome. I have always found the service I received from the company to be no less than excellent. Phil Moulton, Director, has always been exemplary in his professionalism and the high standards he maintains is clearly apparent amongst all the staff he has supplied. During the recent World Track Championships, which took place at the Velodrome (March 2008), I requested high calibre security staff at one day's notice. The purpose was to ensure a Royal visit went smoothly. Despite the short notice, Mr Moulton was able to supply the staff I needed and they performed their duties extremely well. It was certainly a great comfort to me to know that I was able to call upon such a resource when I really needed it. I am delighted to provide a reference for Phil Moulton, and would be happy to be approached for a personal recommendation, if so required.

Jarl Walsh

General Manager Manchester Velodrome

# CHAPTER 21

## 2008 UEFA Cup Final

A couple of months after the royal visit I was tasked to support Manchester City Football Club, who were hosting the 2008 UEFA Cup Final between Zenit Saint Petersburg and Glasgow Rangers.

My role was to assist and organise the logistics and personal security for the VIPs and the UEFA Cup trophy.

We were given the routes and arrival times, and also the number of VIPs that needed moving around. Our first task was to visit the private air terminal at Manchester Airport, then time the route from the airport to the venue in the centre of Manchester. This was carried out on a busy weekend so we would experience the worst-case scenario with the traffic.

We then contacted the airport security to gain the relevant airside clearance for ourselves and the transport - we used a number of MPV type vehicles. Nearer the time all the drivers came together for vehicle familiarisation and to ensure they understood the routes. We then carried out a number of drills, including embussing and debussing, driving in convoys, and use of radio communications.

The main objective of our task was to ensure that the VIPs and the trophy arrived on time. On the day of the event, the entire group arrived at the venue, then deployed to the airport, where security was briefed and all registration numbers, driver's names and contact numbers handed over.

Once we had arrived at the air terminal I informed the organisers from UEFA and Manchester City that everything was going to plan. Once we had confirmation of the flight coming in, 15,10 and 5-minute warnings were given.

Once the flight and party had arrived we passed the information on and the convoy set off. We had put in place a colour code system that identified choke points along the route. As we got nearer to the venue the calls became more frequent, right up to the last two minutes. This enabled us to ensure that the welcoming group were ready. The handover went like clockwork, and the trophy was passed over in a secure and controlled fashion.

Once the final was over and the trophy presented, the event finished and the VIPs were then taken back to the airport. We carried out the exact same operation but in reverse, this time keeping the flight tower informed of our movements, which enabled them to fit the flight into a tight time frame.

The job was a great success and Sara Billington, Head of Operations at Manchester City wrote the following reference in 2009:

In my role as Head of Operations for Manchester City Football Club I had reason to deal with Exclusafe for a number of different functions. Both Phil Moulton and his company are extremely flexible and prepared to assist in any way possible.

The main duties they undertook during my time at the Club were personal security for the Chairman and senior representatives at the football club, providing a number of stewards on a matchday or major event and more importantly as drivers, as and when required.

During 2007 and 2008 Exclusafe worked very closely with my team on the UEFA Cup Final project, ensuring we had vehicles and security throughout the planning process and the event itself. All agencies involved in the organisation had nothing but positive things to say about Phil and his team.

Phil prides himself on being flexible and ensuring the client receives the best service possible. He will ensure plans are in place and that you are totally involved in his preparations and will assist should information be rather vague from the client (which could be quite frequent). Nothing is ever too much trouble and was always available at extremely short notice. When I dealt with Exclusafe they always delivered which took a huge amount of pressure from myself.

Sara Billington

Head of Operations

Manchester City Football Club

# CHAPTER 22

## FOOTBALL LEGENDS

In August 2011 I was asked to provide protection at Manchester's Lowry Hotel by a former member of my staff. The request was to provide protection for the former Manchester United player, Eric Cantona. At the time I was unaware that job would have a duel role, one which would also involve protecting a client that I had previously guarded before.

On arrival we were given a briefing by the close protection team leader. He had experience of protecting high profile clients, and was also a former member of the elite Special Boat Service (SBS).

Our brief was to shadow the client, but not to interfere with his personal space, and also to make sure that he felt safe and wasn't bothered by the public. The role included providing basic escort duties around the hotel. My familiarisation with the hotel, the staff, and members of the paparazzi, helped the situation.

Eric Cantona's visit was due to a friendly match between New York Cosmos and Manchester United. It was also a testimonial match for the Manchester United player, Paul Scholes, and Cantona was managing the Cosmos team.

As the security team who were looking after him were from out of town, I acted as a link between them and the venue. This involved contacting Manchester United to arrange a quick recce for the head of security. I took them there in my car and outlined the routes, while Eric was tucked up in the hotel. They were completely shocked how fast I organised things for them and the plan went well.

During the time I was with Eric Cantona I basically watched the crowd and ensured that he was not bothered. I think he felt easy with me around him, and I did feel he trusted my actions. He is a private man with a great presence, and was a pleasure to work with.

Below is a letter I received from Jason Morse, Player Liaison Officer at New York Cosmos:

'Phil, it was good to hear from you and it gives me a chance to say thanks again for your professionalism and dedication during our recent visit to Manchester.

I hope that you have a successful meeting tomorrow with Blackburn and if there is anything I can do for you last minute, please don't hesitate to call my mobile.

I agree that networking within this community is critical, and I believe that Football clubs especially, require some unique attention and detail that only experience can bring.'

While working with the New York Cosmos and Eric Cantona, I also encountered one of my old clients – the Brazilian football legend, Pele.

I had looked after him a few years before while he was on a previous visit to Manchester, and this time I had been asked to ask him if he would sign a football shirt. When I approached him he recognised me, gave me a massive hug and said 'It's you, how are you?'

The people around us looked shocked as nobody had known I knew him or had looked after him before.

He signed the shirt and then gave me signed a picture, which I cherish.

With the football legend and great man, Pele

My first encounter with Pele was back in 1998, it came after I got a request from a client who provide chauffeurs for VIPs. The brief was that Pele would visit a number of venues before attending the opening of the Manchester United Museum, which had moved to the newly redeveloped North Stand.

The job itself was quite easy, the only real issue we had was that the Spice Girls were also in town, and because Pele was travelling in a white stretch limo, we attracted some unwanted attention!

On the day we went to the stadium and followed the drills that I'd put in place, making the warning calls as we were travelling in the limo with Pele, Simon Marsh from Umbro, and a few others in the back. I had already encountered the head of security at Old Trafford, but for whatever reason he'd said that I wasn't allowed to go into the stadium.

When we arrived, the security was 'all singing, all dancing, with bells and whistles!' Pele and his party left us and went into the stadium, while I waited with the limo. While the event was on, a large crowd had gathered outside. When Pele and his party came back out after it had finished, I had expected the same level of security, but instead there was none. As the crowd swarmed over us we had to hustle Pele into the car, at which point the driver, Roy Power, god bless him, asked where the security was!

By this stage the limo was surrounded by the crowd and was being rocked from side to side. With no sign of any security I had no option but to get out of the car and walk in front, clearing the area with no support whatsoever. I was shouting at the top of my voice and the crowd became a bit subdued and started to move out of the way. There were no more issues apart from some worried folk in the back of the limo.

Once we got back to the hotel it was supposed to be relax time, but the party were very shaken, in fact the head of the party went home looking very shook up, and left it for me to deal with.

We grabbed some lunch only to get a call asking us to head back to the hotel to take Pele and the party to a restaurant. We had arranged a table at very high-class venue called the Mash and Air, but on arrival Pele looked at me and asked if I knew anywhere better!

I knew an Italian restaurant on George Street on the edge of Manchester's Chinatown. When we arrived, I went into the restaurant asked for a table for seven people, checked the area, and escorted the legendary Pele inside. You can only imagine their faces, but the owners were brilliant. Pele enjoyed the meal, signed a plate and left feeling very happy - a happy ending to a bad morning.

The main issues we encountered on that job was the sheer number of professional autograph hunters. They constantly followed and harassed the group and always seemed to know where and when we were going.

Because I had carried out a full recce of the venues, I was able to work out which entry and exit points to use. This wasn't exactly a life-threatening situation but it did cause the group a number of problems. Every day we used different debussing points and random times, which helped us to control the situation.

At the end of the job, and still being followed and harassed by the autograph hunters, we arrived at the airport. I met the police and was just about to pass Pele over for safe passage through to customs, when Roy

Power asked him to sign a rolled-up newspaper – I was gobsmacked!

I consider myself very fortunate to have looked after the great Pele on three occasions, first of all in1998, then 2005 and finally in 2011 - which was a special one for me because it was my birthday!

# CHAPTER 23

## BLACKBURN ROVERS FOOTBALL CLUB

In 2011 I was asked by Blackburn Rovers Football Club to assist with the security of some training ground issues, and also the protection of Steve Kean, the football manager.

Prior to this role developing I was asked to go with the club to India on a pre-season PR visit. At the time there had been no recce carried out, so as always, our first job was to gather intelligence about the visit, the area, and even the client. After some internal issues a recce was carried out by another person who had some police experience, but the information provided was very basic.

My responsibility was to escort the management, players and their wives. I did this alongside a group of armed police and a private security company.

The owners of the club are very security conscious, the main concerns were that the roads were very heavy with traffic, and also the lack of traffic management in the area. The other major issue was that there had been an explosion in Mumbai only a few weeks before the visit, and we were the first Premier League club to visit the area in a number of years.

The security in the compound, which was the Marriot Hotel in Pune, was acceptable, we had armed protection at the hotel, and security on every floor.

The biggest threat was when we were moving around Pune. We were in a large coach, with the owner's name and the club's advertisement emblazoned all over it, so on a target-based situation, we were high profile. But saying that, the support from both the owners influence and the police, was very good and the visit went off without any major issues.

After returning from India my role with the club grew. I was brought in sometimes at the very last minute under the instruction of the safety manager. On those occasions it was to deal with protests that had been taking place at the training ground. Although there was no violence involved, at times there were between 50-70 protestors outside the gates, which at times was quite intimidating to the club's players and staff.

This issue was also a problem on match days and the protection of Steve Kean, the manager, wasn't the best.

Before my involvement there was an occasion when a supporter had got onto the pitch.

There was also an occasion when Steve was out at a restaurant with his family, when a friend messaged him to say his location had been revealed on social media and an activist group was encouraging people to confront him. He made the wise choice to leave. There was also a suggestion that he had been followed home from a match and also the training ground.

The protests on match days grew and the groups were well organized. Although there were no physical attacks the atmosphere at the games was at times very aggressive, and for the manager it was very difficult.

There was quite a lot of things that went on behind the closed doors with Steve. Some of the protestors were from a group called the Blackburn Rovers Action Group, they were a well organised group, who although troublesome, never really gave me any issues. The crowd on the other hand, gave him stick for the full ninety minutes of the match. They chanted 'Kean Out', and he had some real problems, it was difficult for him, but to his credit, he handled it very well.

I travelled quite a lot with him, to India, Holland, Ireland, and across the UK. It was an active job which required a great deal of concentration. When he wasn't at matches, he was at the training ground, where extra vigilance was required.

The bonus on that job was that Steve was very open to security and had a positive approach to accepting protection. That made life easier for me as a protection officer. I was with him for twelve months, right up until he left the club in 2012.

The main problems I encountered however was from inside the club. Venky's, the Indian conglomerate that owned Blackburn Rovers, appointed me as their Chief of Security after an incident where the owners suffered humiliation – they had been pelted by snowballs by disgruntled fans. But the reality was that the real threat to them came from within the club – a threat that came from high-up and which included most, if not all of the security team.

Guarding a person is one thing, but trying to control the very people who are trusted by the owners, from causing the issues, is a different matter entirely.

Because the owners were not in the country all the time, when they did visit, there was a great deal of protest and a lot of animosity.

During my time at the club I had looked after a number of areas of safety and security, and after a period of time they had started to adopt the right SOPs.

It is these SOPs that are crucial for the protection of the client, and the surrounding people.

I parted company with Blackburn Rovers in 2014, but my biggest regret was that in taking the job with the club it effectively ended my involvement with the Football Association. The details behind that situation is another story, and maybe one day I'll tell it.

While writing this book Steve Kean very kindly wrote the following:

The first time I had contact with Phil was on our trip with the squad to India. Beforehand, Phil had looked after all the personal security for the owners when they had visited home games at Blackburn Rovers. This trip was a big logistical job, not only because of the distance but also the commitments the staff and the players had to undertake whilst in India as well as playing a match. Phil was superb, always calm, very professional and gave us a feeling of being safe in a highly excited and highly populated area of the world.

Coming from the East End of Glasgow, and that is a tough part of the UK, I never thought that I would need a personal body guard beside me, certainly not whilst working in the English Premier League. This was the owner's idea and as I learned, it is a very common practice in India for people to have personal protection both in the work place and in their private life outside of their job.

I found it very easy to work with Phil because I always felt that he was ahead of what might happen next and his planning was meticulous. For example, if I was having the final session of the week before travelling to an away game, Phil would pick me up at my house at 6.30 am, we would go to the training ground and be the first to arrive, Phil would check all the areas to ensure the training ground was safe for the players, staff and I. If we had an away game after that session, we would immediately leave the training ground after the session and Phil had all the protocols in place to ensure that all the players, staff and I would get to the train station, board the train, have maximum security whilst on the train, leave the train and board the coach at our destination then get to the hotel safely before checking in. At first, I thought 'this seems a bit over the top' but now, looking back and seeing the measures and detail to planning that he had put in place to maintain safety, I now know that this was top class work.

Phil was a very interesting guy to talk to and I got to know him and his family well. I think because of Phil's extremely high level of personal training, i.e. his karate grading as well as his accreditation for looking after groups of people 24/7 gives him a totally different perspective from the normal man or woman on the street going about their daily life. He appears to have a sixth sense and anticipates potential danger before it happens. This ability is incredible to see at first hand and he diffuses potential problems before they happen. I think he does this subconsciously or maybe it's just that he is on call every minute of every day. As a result of this I have never seen him using physical means to resolve a situation.

When I had finished my working day at the training ground, normally around 7.00 pm, Phil taught me the basic katas of the first two karate belts. This was tough but very enjoyable and fortunately to this day, I have never had the need to use the skills he passed on to me.

Some of the fans were angry and restless. The Club was in a period of transition. The previous owners had spent millions of pounds to win the Premier League and now the Club had new owners. Not being a football man, Phil would ask me 'why are the fans not happy today, we just won'. It was hard for me to explain to him.

To sum Phil up as a Close Protection Professional, I would say he will always see danger before it happens, has a great ability to diffuse potential danger and guide the person/people he is looking after to safety. He gives you confidence and you feel that no matter what is out there, you're safe. He plans then counter plans, this in itself shows that he is never complacent.

As a man, he is calm, very easy going, extremely funny and has time not only for the bosses of the organisation but also the workers who are sometimes overlooked. He has great integrity and I'll always be grateful for the time we spent together. He really is a top man!

# CHAPTER 24

## STAY TRUE TO YOURSELF

Losing our company, Exclusafe, in 2010-11, after ten very successful years had a bad effect on me and my family – we were devastated. Having built up a list of clients which most companies could only wish for - we lost it all almost overnight.

My wife took ill due to the stress and worry of losing our home, and seeing her suffer day in day out nearly destroyed me as a person. I take full responsibility for it, I made the wrong choices, rushed into too many things and now have many regrets about some of the decisions I took. However, there is always two sides to a story and there are a number of factors around some of those decisions that I haven't detailed in this book. Someday it would be fantastic to say what really happened, and by who...

Now in 2018, I am working to support my family, and we are re-building our lives. I have re-launched my karate classes and still teaching close protection courses to students which include: novices, VIP bodyguards, the Royal Military Police and former members of the British SAS – something I am very proud of.

I started life with a mission to be a success, and despite the challenges that have been thrown at me, I made it to the top of my sport and profession, proof that if you work hard enough, and have the desire and commitment, anything is possible.

My dream was to teach others how to look after themselves, and also to protect people who were being bullied or intimidated. I have had the privilege of protecting people from all over the world, some were famous, while others were just ordinary folk with ordinary families. There is nothing more rewarding then knowing a person and their loved ones are safe due to the things you've put in place.

I consider myself very fortunate to have been able to do this and grateful for the privilege of protecting stars from the world of sport and entertainment, safeguarding members of international organisations, and advising and training government agencies, corporations and the military.

I have had the honour of working with clients from around the world, including Russia, USA, Denmark, Sweden and Spain - operating alongside former members of British Special Forces, the French Secrete, and the Spanish Guardia Civil.

From the experience gained through karate and in close protection, I have been able to pass on my knowledge and skills to over 2500 students. Teaching them an array of subjects including: Close Protection, Surveillance and Counter Surveillance, Conflict Management, Arrest and Restraint, Armed and Unarmed Close Quarter Combat, and Personal Safety.

Many of those students have gone on themselves to become established protection officers, some travelling the world with their own companies. Helping others was and still is my dream, and there is no better feeling than having a positive influence on someone's life.

To those who have been in my position a thought for you. Remember in life people can take things away - contracts, business, even friends - but one thing they can't ever take is YOU.

Stay true to yourself, and your goals in life will be achieved, no matter what.

Printed in Poland
by Amazon Fulfillment
Poland Sp. z o.o., Wrocław